UNIVERSITY OF NORTH CAROLINA
STUDIES IN THE ROMANCE LANGUAGES AND LITERATURES
Number 60

THE LITERARY PERSPECTIVISM OF
RAMÓN PÉREZ DE AYALA

THE LITERARY PERSPECTIVISM OF
RAMÓN PÉREZ DE AYALA

BY

FRANCES WYERS WEBER

CHAPEL HILL

THE UNIVERSITY OF NORTH CAROLINA PRESS

PRINTED IN SPAIN

DEPÓSITO LEGAL: V. 452 - 1966

ARTES GRÁFICAS SOLER, S. A. - VALENCIA - 1966

TABLE OF CONTENTS

	Page
INTRODUCTION. An Ideological Portrait	11
CHAPTER I. The Shifting Perspective of the Narrator	23
— II. The Multiple Perspectives of the Characters. *Belarmino y Apolonio*	49
— III. Linguistic Perspectivism	67
— IV. Reality and Art	88

To Enrique Anderson Imbert

The publication of this work was made possible through a grant from the Horace H. Rackham School of Graduate Studies, the University of Michigan.

INTRODUCTION: AN IDEOLOGICAL PORTRAIT

During the twenty three years of his active literary life (1903-1926), Ramón Pérez de Ayala wrote poetry, literary essays, criticism, novels, and short stories. His fiction is notably intellectual. It develops and illustrates such speculative problems as the nature and kinds of knowledge, the ambiguity of language, and the role of art in interpreting the world. Since the novelist's theoretical interests so clearly determine the subject, style, and structure of his imaginative works, a brief review of his ideas, based largely on the essays, is a useful introduction to an examination of the fiction. The main part of this study will be an analysis of the transformation of conceptual topics into novelistic form. The principle of organization will be a grouping of techniques that reflect certain central and persistent themes.

One of the most noticeable characteristics of Pérez de Ayala's composition is the use of a dual or multiple focus on events, persons, things, and ideas—a focus that successively shows opposing facets and attitudes. In order to achieve a prismatic image of reality, he brings together incompatible theories, lists discrepant opinions about a given fact, varies the emotional distance between narrator and event or presents the action from two widely separated points of view. He may build a scene on the different connotations of a word, or shift between the planes of reality and fantasy, transposing life into artistic representation. Through ironic qualification, he undermines the illusory stability of characters and ideas, and through antitheses, paradoxes, word-plays, and puns, he points up the dubious reliability of words. He exaggerates linguistic ambiguity by creating individual speech styles and by introducing characters who invent private, hermetic languages.

But this tendency to shatter the continuity of reality into myriad discrete fragments is met by a counter-tendency to impose order and harmony: opposites must be united, antitheses resolved. Significantly, his ideal in literature is classicism, which he defines not as a historical style but as an eternal standard for the balance of centripetal and centrifugal impulses to represent inner and outer worlds. Classicism is the integration of spirit and matter, poetry and reality, subjectivity and objectivity.

These contrary aims and techniques are the result of Pérez de Ayala's attitude towards knowledge and reality: he believes that knowledge is relative but that there is, nevertheless, a single absolute reality beyond the reach of human reason. He envisions an ultimate cosmic harmony that perfectly reconciles all conflicts and contradictions; although man cannot rationally grasp this total reality, he can intuit it through esthetic experience, imitate it in a work of art, affirm and revere it in the practice of tolerance. In his fiction, these two disparate conceptions, a relativistic theory of knowledge and a belief in an absolute, balanced reality, suggest themes and determine composition; in some works the first dominates, in others the second, and occasionally they seem to collide and conflict.

The Perspectivism of Knowledge

For Pérez de Ayala, the world discovered by reason is one in which all hypotheses are equally cogent and equally unverifiable. Implicitly denying all fixed criteria of truth, he asserts that each individual perspective is true. Truth would seem to be infinite: it can be identified with each and every theory under the sun. *Belarmino y Apolonio* is the fictional realization of this relativism. After illustrating, through the novel's action, opposing approaches to knowledge, life, language, drama, philosophy, and the art of the novel, the narrator explains that all antitheses are linked by a continuum of partial truths that stretches between them:

> Tan verdad puede ser lo de don Amaranto como lo de Escobar; y entre la verdad de Escobar y la de don Amaranto se extienden sinnúmero infinito de otras verdades intermedias, que es lo que los matemáticos llaman *ultra-*

continuo. Hay tantas verdades irreducibles como puntos de vista (p. 193).

Some critics have remarked on the similarity between Pérez de Ayala's idea of a multifaceted reality apprehended through numberless unique points of view and the perspectivism of Ortega y Gasset.[1] Both Ortega and the novelist consider truth to be the sum of individual perspectives;[2] error is the arrogant assumption that any single theory can embrace reality in its entirety: "El error es de aquellos que piden que una opinión humana posea verdad absoluta. Basta que encierre un polvillo o una pepita de verdad" (*Belarmino*, 193).[3] Both Ortega y Gasset and Pérez de Ayala move from the notion of the fragmentation of truth to that of the deficiency of each fragment (a position inconsistent with thoroughgoing relativism).[4] The partial truth must be enlarged, for its partiality is a form of falsity: "Hay una forma de falsedad, que consiste en el enunciado a medias de una verdad" (*Divagaciones*, p. 217). Each perspective shows only a tiny portion of reality, and although all perspectives are equally true, the necessary limitation of each point of view is itself a distortion. Man must constantly strive to uncover complementary or contra-

---

[1] Mariano Baquero Goyanes, in "La novela como tragicomedia: Pérez de Ayala y Ortega," *Insula,* 110 (1955), p. 4, discusses the idea of the novel as defined by Ortega and practiced by Pérez de Ayala. He calls attention to similarities between the two writers: "Me gustaría estudiar... lo que de orteguiano hay en Pérez de Ayala, sobre todo, su gusto por el perspectivismo, convertido en procedimiento novelesco, descriptivo, analizador... y junto al gusto por los efectos perspectivísticos, cabría señalar las relativamente abundantes páginas novelescas de Pérez de Ayala sobre algo que si no es la 'razón vital' de Ortega, se le aproxima bastante. A lo largo de *Los trabajos de Urbano y Simona,* y sobre todo, en las encendidas palabras que el tema de la 'razón vital' suscita en Colás al final de *El curandero de su honra* pueden encontrarse ejemplos muy expresivos."

[2] "La verdad integral sólo se obtiene articulando lo que el prójimo ve con lo que yo veo y así sucesivamente. *Cada individuo es un punto de vista esencial.* Yuxtaponiendo las visiones parciales de todos se lograría tejer la verdad omnímoda y absoluta." José Ortega y Gasset, *El tema de nuestro tiempo* (Madrid, 1923), p. 157.

[3] "La sola perspectiva falsa es la que pretende ser la única." *Ibid.,* p. 152.

[4] "Vemos los errores como verdades incompletas, parciales..., tienen razón *en parte.*" Ortega y Gasset, "2.500 años y un solo filósofo," *La Gaceta* (June, 1960), p. 1. The conflict between Ortega's relativism and his absolutistic axiology parallels the conflict between Pérez de Ayala's perspectivism and his metaphysical absolutism.

dictory aspects of the world and then attempt to combine these dualities into larger units of understanding:

> La verdad flota atomizada y desperdigada por el mundo. La inteligencia procura reunir y conciliar el mayor número de estas verdades fragmentarias, heterogéneas, y por lo común contradictorias. La inteligencia que rehuye este esfuerzo de unidad y concentración y se deja a la merced de los usos cambiantes y espejismos de las infinitas lentejuelas en que la verdad aparece subdividida, concluye ella misma atomizándose, dispersándose, evaporándose, volatilizándose... Ante las medias verdades y múltiples facetas de la realidad, debemos proceder con tacto y reserva. Hasta tanto que no hemos descubierto otras nuevas facetas complementarias de este puro y diáfano diamante de la verdad (*Divagaciones*, pp. 217-18). [5]

But although Pérez de Ayala here seems to be suggesting the possibility of eventually reconstructing the "diaphanous diamond" of truth out of its atomized bits, he does not really believe that the methods of reason can ever lead to total knowledge; the universe must remain forever hidden to the intellect: "Cada época enfoca al universo desde un vértice de óptica diferente. Los problemas esenciales de la vida, aunque siempre los mismos, están planteados en términos nuevos, ya la eterna incógnita recibe diversa denominación en cada época" (*Divagaciones*, p. 214). He does not imagine a progressive increase of human understanding through the continual merging of antitheses. One tries to bring together as many contrary interpretations as possible, not in order to build a single, gigantic rational whole but, rather, in order to display multiplicity itself. [6]

---

[5] Using a similar image, Ortega envisions truth splintered into infinite shards: "Diríase que la razón se hizo añicos antes de empezar el hombre a pensar, y por eso, tiene éste que ir recogiendo los pedazos uno a uno a juntarlos. ...reconozcamos que aquella verdad manca, convicta de error, desaparece en la nueva construcción intelectual. Pero desaparece porque es asimilada en otra más completa... Superadas en otras más complejas, es lo que Hegel llamaba *aufhebung*." (Loc. cit.)

[6] Ortega, on the other hand, as the above reference to Hegel might have led us to suspect, does believe that philosophy gradually increases the sum of man's knowledge: "La serie de los filósofos aparece como un solo filósofo que hubiera vivido 2.500 años." (*Loc. cit.*)

Being: Absolutism

Pérez de Ayala conceives ultimate reality as a concord of infinite antagonisms. The contradictions that reason can never resolve become, when considered from the remote, inhuman perspective of the Absolute, necessary and complementary parts of the real. Duality is then revealed as an essential feature of reality, for the harmony of the universe reconciles and balances all opposites without obliterating their distinction. Sometimes, personifying this universal equilibrium, Pérez de Ayala speaks of a Creator who, although he loves and justifies all his creatures, has made them in such a way that they clash and destroy one another:

> Observamos que en la creación cada ser y cada cosa, tomados individualmente, obedece a una fatalidad que le ha sido impuesta; cada ser y cada cosa no es sino la manera aparente de obrar de un principio elemental, cuya última raíz se alimenta de la sustancia misteriosa del Creador... El lobo es antipático a la oveja, y la oveja es antipática al lobo. Pero con perspectiva dilatada; más arriba aún de la estrella Sirio... desde el manantial de origen, oveja y lobo son amables en la misma medida (*Máscaras*, I, 72).

This reference to a *Creador* in no way implies belief in a transcendent God, a God separated from his creation and therefore one more element in a dualistic series.[7] In Pérez de Ayala's radically monistic metaphysics, there is nothing other than the whole of Creation, self-sufficient in its stability and perfection. But usually he expresses this monism in mechanical terms, describing the universe as a delicate system of counterweights and balances:

---

[7] Norma Urrutia, in *De Troteras a Tigre Juan* (Madrid, 1960), p. 29, refers to the religious tone of much of this author's writing: "Se diría que el pensamiento de Ayala es un pensamiento religioso, no obstante su crítica casi continua de la Iglesia; situación ésta que se da con frecuencia entre los españoles, para quienes, por razones históricas, la Iglesia aparece más como un poder temporal que divino y eterno." Pérez de Ayala believes that God is a creation of man's aspirations and longings: in a poem titled "La Ilusión," he gives several definitions of illusion and among them we find "Dios" and "Madre de Dios." *Poesías completas* (Buenos Aires, 1942), pp. 101, 102.

> Cuanto más se acusen las diversas personalidades y con más claridad se defina la oposición, con tanta mayor naturalidad sobrevendrá la solución o el equilibrio de tendencias y leyes entre sí adversas, de donde se concierta la gran armonía universal (*Máscaras*, I, 76-77).

The finite, experienced world of shifting appearances and ceaseless flux is nothing but a manifestation or derivation of the infinite, and if we imaginatively consider it as such, this realm of time and of change is suddenly congealed into a complex network of eternal, inextricable relationships:

> Todo es fugitivo, / todo es efímero, / ante el Infinito. / Pero al tiempo mismo, / todo es divino; / cabos, hebras, hilos / de un solo ovillo, / el Infinito. / En un nudo se enlazan innumerables hilos. / En el punto que pisas, / se cruzan todos los caminos. / Todo es necesario y todo es preciso (*Poesías*, 129).

Once the duality of the finite world is seen as both inevitable and illusory, values, especially moral ones, become relative. The author's moral relativism springs not from his perspectivistic theory of knowledge but from the metaphysical assumption of a world in which good cannot exist without evil:

> Las cosas son buenas miradas por la cara, y malas miradas por el envés, o viceversa. Por el equilibrio inestable se produce el equilibrio estable... El espíritu liberal y el espíritu faccioso, Dios y el Diablo... se darán al fin y a la postre el abrazo de Vergara. Diré aún más. En la penumbra de la conciencia del hombre se abrazan el Bien y el Mal (*Máscaras*, I, 81).

Individual acts of merit or blame are not the result of human will for they depend solely on one's function in a total design: "¿Qué culpa tuvo Judas? Judas era necesario, era imprescindible, era uno de los contrarios que entraban en la combinación de la tragedia del Gólgota" (*Máscaras*, I, 77). Pérez de Ayala's metaphysical intuition thus leads to an ethical outlook entirely consistent with the relativism of his theory of knowledge. And his value system, in turn, plays an important part in his picture of the universe, for the virtue of tolerance enables one to apprehend ultimate reality.

The precise order of reality is not for Pérez de Ayala a mere subjective hypothesis; it is an objective fact, albeit a fact inaccessible to the intellect. Rationality does not lead to total knowledge for it deals with only a small portion of experience. The limitations of reason are evident in the contrast between the analytical functions of science and the synthetic comprehension made possible by theology in earlier, more ingenuous times. In *Belarmino y Apolonio*, one of the characters, Don Amaranto de Fraile, traces the increasing restrictions of the mind's field of vision: originally matter and spirit were firmly conjoined in thought, but the rise of rationalism destroyed this notion of wholeness, consigning to reason a physical world devoid of transcendence and meaning and relegating to religion a desembodied spirituality. The sciences further fragment the material world by multiplying their disciplines until each single object examined explodes into millions of images and incoherent facts.[8] In view of the failure of both science and religion, Don Amaranto proposes that in our day the only modes of knowledge or creation capable of integrating experience are philosophy (metaphysics) and drama.

The author would agree with his character that in order to understand life fully, one must approach it with other than rational procedures. If conceptual thought is necessarily relative, only intuition can enable man to grasp the whole of reality. And

---

[8] "La edad científica sigue a la edad teológica. Es decir, cuando la humanidad, tras haber imaginado penetrar el sentido de la vida y la muerte... volvió sobre sí y, con maravilla y espanto, descubrió... que la vida no tiene sentido ni el orbe consiente que se le abarque; en aquel traste lastimoso que fue algo así como una almoneda en donde se desbarató el hogar y menaje de los dioses, algunos individuos remataron a bajo precio tales y cuales trastos de la almoneda, que aunque apolillados y claudicantes, todavía duran y se utilizan, y otros individuos, muy contados, más propensos a la desesperanza y al tedio, volviéronse de espaldas al cielo, ya vacío y desalquilado, humillaron los ojos hacia el suelo, y aplicáronse a reunir por semejas hechos minúsculos... y así se fue formando cada una de las ciencias particulares" (*Belarmino*, pp. 11-12). According to Don Amaranto "en la edad teológica, el hombre se había acostumbrado a la presencia de lo absoluto en cada realidad relativa; el mundo estaba poblado de mitos; la esencia de los seres flotaba en la superficie, como la niebla matinal sobre los ríos; y el conocimiento íntegro se ofrecía al alcance de la mano, como la frambuesa de los setos" (p. 12). On the other hand, "con penetrar un poco en todas las ciencias, así puras como aplicadas, se descompone al punto una imagen en millares de imágenes" (pp. 12-13).

intuition, for Pérez de Ayala, is a concomitant both of the virtue of tolerance and of the esthetic emotion, for each frees the individual from the confines of his solitary point of view. Curiously, he makes esthetic and ethical values interdependent and almost interchangeable. Moral comprehension and tolerance derive from sensibility and imagination: "sin sentidos y sin imaginación, la simpatía falta; y sin pasar por la simpatía no se llega al amor; sin amor no puede haber comprensión moral; y sin comprensión moral no hay tolerancia". [9] Esthetic appreciation arises from empathy, the precondition of tolerance:

> El hecho estético esencial es... la confusión (fundirse con) o transfusión (fundirse en) de uno mismo en los demás y aun en los seres inanimados, y aun en los fenómenos físicos, y aun en los más simples esquemas o figuras geométricas; vivir por entero en la medida de lo posible las emociones ajenas; y a los seres inanimados henchirlos y saturarlos de emoción, "personificarlos". (*Troteras*, p. 145).

The catharsis of tragedy prepares one for the exercise of tolerance and justice ("las dos más grandes virtudes, y estoy por decir que las únicas," *Ibid.*, p. 294). Thus the impulses that enable man to transcend empirical knowledge are so intimately related that it is difficult to separate them entirely: through disinterested artistic contemplation, one transforms conflicts into a pleasing arrangement of balanced forces, and this vision, in turn, predisposes one to the moral acceptance of all opposites. In art and in the practice of tolerance, man perceives and recreates the harmony of the world.

Art and Absolute Reality

The novelist sees in his craft the possibility of an almost mystical illumination: through it one can catch sight of the order of the universe. Esthetic emotion, like religious ecstasy, converts the

---

[9] *Troteras*, p. 144. The speaker is the semi-autobiographical hero of the novel, Alberto Díaz de Guzmán; that he is the theoretical mouth-piece of the author is evident in the extensive quotations from this novel that Pérez de Ayala includes in his essays on the drama in *Las máscaras*, II.

disorder of experience into meaningful beauty: in a description of the effects of poetry on man's understanding of the world, he adapts a phrase of Fray Luis de León:

> El mundo se transfigura y serena, es lo que fue en su origen: *mundo*, que vale tanto como belleza, pulcritud y orden; *universo*, todo convergiendo a uno, la palabra fecunda, el *verbo* melodioso, harmonioso y preñado de sentido eterno como un verso solo y único (*Divagaciones*, 118-19).

The rapt attention which is elicited by the work of art nullifies one's awareness of the schism between the self and the world: consciousness transcends itself and achieves an illusion of wholeness (Pérez de Ayala's paradoxical words are "ensimismarse enajenándose").[10] This momentary convergence of subject and object points to a universal conciliation of opposites.

Not only does Pérez de Ayala consider esthetic experience a means of access to ultimate reality but, confusing the emotional effect of a work of art with its interior structure, he asserts that the latter is a picture or mirror of universal harmony. This confusion is particularly evident in his conception of drama and the novel, which he praises as faithful reproductions, not of the hazards and changefulness of the world we live in, but of its perfect order:

> Novela y drama son las únicas formas de arte que corresponden con la vida, tomada ésta en toda su integridad... en la novela y el drama, la vida, y su marco el universo, se contienen tales como son, por entero y en su armonía suprema. Y así, si hay algún arte que deba llevar el nombre de creación, será la novela o el drama, porque uno y otro son como epítome y trasunto compendiado de la gran creación divina (*Máscaras*, I, 69).

Pérez de Ayala believes that the novelist imposes on life a rational scheme of causality and intention, that he transmutes meaningless

---

[10] "Abolir el universo real circunstancialmente, en tanto que uno se absorbe en la ficción de la vida interior, con que agitarse y colmarse a sí propio, es decir, a sí mismo, esto no es sino ensimismarse. Pero ensimismarse enajenándose; antinomia que es una identidad, como la mayoría de las antinomias" (*Divagaciones*, p. 77).

chance into intelligible design. But so impressed is our author with the novel's inner coherence, that he concludes it must in some way derive from the total congruence of the universe. Because he considers the literary work a pale reflection of the absolute order, he often tries to sharpen that effect in the novel: through the symmetrical arrangement of incidents or through a rather forced final reconciliation, he makes orderliness the most salient feature. Description and theory pass easily into precept. The ideal of harmony not only furnishes a model to be copied but also gives the novel an extra-literary, moral significance. Again we note the characteristic fusion of esthetic concept and moral value: the novelist, by representing a plan of creation wherein all warring forces are necessary and just, instructs his readers in tolerance:

> ¿Qué otra cosa son los grandes novelistas y dramaturgos sino... intérpretes, aunque falibles, de un presunto plan providente que rige los destinos mortales; vates, o zahoríes de la armonía universal, y, por ende, sacerdotes de la universal tolerancia? (*Divagaciones*, p. 150).

The Theorist as Novelist

The most important configurative element in Pérez de Ayala's mature fiction is perspectivism. We shall see how the counter-tendency towards symmetry and stability modifies and at times distorts his relativism. In either ideological tendency, the writer is concerned with his own role: amid innumerable conflicting views, the novelist himself becomes coordinator and commentator or, confronted with human strife, he steps in to decree concord. The creative activity of the artist, a central theme in all of his novels, is explicitly formulated in the first four, which have as their subject the autobiographic figure of a young writer. Implicitly it is elaborated in the later novels through ingenious contrivances of plot that call attention to the author as fabricator. In a sense, Pérez de Ayala has made of himself a primary object of focus: working out his intellectual suppositions through various narrative devices, he emerges as the protagonist of his own fictions. Because he is more interested in showing the artist creating than the creation itself, he uses the problems of perspectivism and the illusions of fiction as topics to be schematically illustrated. The multiplicity of points of view, the ambiguity of language and of all experience are never thoroughly absorbed or fictionalized. Rather than reproduce the complexity of a world made up out of divergent ideas and explanations of reality, Pérez de Ayala seems to be discussing with the reader the nature and consequences of that complexity. His novels do not so much produce the image of a concrete, three-dimensional world as suggest a two-dimensional projection, like those patterns of parallel and diagonal lines laid out by Renaissance painters as guides for a mathematically correct perspective.

CHAPTER I

THE SHIFTING PERSPECTIVE OF THE NARRATOR

In *La deshumanización del arte* (1925), Ortega y Gasset describes the different perspectives of four people at the death bed of a famous man; after considering the emotional distance between the wife's grief, the doctor's medical concern, the reporter's professional interest, and the purely esthetic attitude of a painter who is present by chance, he concludes that "one and the same reality may split into many diverse realities when it is beheld from different points of view".[1] The analysis that follows classifies these realities on the basis of the spectator's detachment or involvement and ends with a distinction between "lived" and "observed" reality. This little illustrative scene is anticipated by a similar one in Pérez de Ayala's *Troteras y danzaderas* (1913): Teófilo Pajares, a ridiculous and pathetic would-be poet lies dying; the reader has followed his tragicomedy throughout the novel, but now the narrator introduces a totally alien observer, the actor Macías, who "a una distancia prudencial, por temor al contagio, estudiaba la expresión del enfermo, la deformación de sus facciones, sus gestos, ademanes e inflexiones de voz, por si llegaba el caso de representar en escena algún moribundo de granujía, que todo podía ocurrir" (p. 370).

Pérez de Ayala often views his fictional creatures with the same remote gaze; divesting them of life and will, he regards them functionally as ingredients for the composition of the story. His role as novelist holds him apart from the events of the plot

---

[1] José Ortega y Gasset, *Obras Completas* (Madrid, 1950), III, 361.

and leads him to think of the living models for his characters in an inhuman, utilitarian way. The dramas of real people are raw materials for art:

> Me había acostumbrado a tomar las diversas casas de huéspedes, por donde transité, al modo de tiendas, con sus existencias, tal cual abastecidas de dramas individuales, metido cada cual en su paquete y cuidadosamente atados con bramante. No había sino desatar el bramante y desenrollar el paquete. Si aquellas casas eran tiendas de menguado surtido, la de doña Trina destacaba al modo de vasto y rico almacén, con géneros únicos de fabricación única. Verdad que no se podía sacar sino el género; luego se exigía cierta diligencia para darle hechura (*Belarmino*, p. 15).

Human beings are food for the novelist, nourishment for the flesh of his story:

> Entre las personas consagradas a la vida religiosa se encuentran almas de absoluta simplicidad y blandura... se las pudiera llamar almas moluscos... Para un espíritu profundo e inquisitivo tales almas ofrecen deliciosas primicias en el vasto festín de la realidad; algo así como las ostras frescas y vivas para el gastrónomo (*Bajo el signo de Artemisa*, p. 238).

But most frequently this estrangement from his personages is intermitent. The narrator alternates the external focus with an internal one: after giving a brief glimpse of a character's feelings, he destroys the human semblance by showing, in a purely graphic way, the outward physical being. He contrasts inner aspiration and outer reality through shifts from a sympathetic to an ironic view, thereby pointing up the relativity of both subjective and objective interpretations. Several devices fracture the narrator's vision into apparently reverse images: dehumanizing descriptions, the mechanization of action, indirect characterization by physical traits and surroundings, the concrete representation of thoughts and feelings, the inclusion of the story within an essay-like framework, and diametrical polarities of characters and dramatic actions. All are embodiments of the narrator's dual perspective.

Dehumanization

In dehumanizing his characters, the author disengages himself from their drama. So persistent is this technique that everyone in these fictions at one time or another dissolves into simple corporeity; some of the characters, especially secondary ones, never do attain the prestige of human form. Pérez de Ayala is fascinated by what he calls "grotesque" creatures, anomalies on the evolutionary scale, half-human, half-inhuman (*Máscaras* II, 240). Lowest in the hierarchy is a woman like Prisca, the maid in *La caída de los Limones*; she is nothing more than an assemblage of geometrical shapes by which the author signifies that "no daba impresión de criatura racional, ni aun irracional ... era más bien una cosa, en cuya forma aparente se representaban ciertos caracteres simbólicos: la solidez, la exactitud..." (*Prometeo*, p. 226). In *Tinieblas en las cumbres*, the image of Cerdá is equally inanimate but more grotesque; certain facial features are separated from the whole and given a lowly life of their own: "No podéis imaginaros obra de mampostería tan complicada y admirable como la cabeza del señor Cerdá... las cejas como dos porquetas o cucarachas que pasearan por el tal obelisco" (p. 22). Higher on the evolutionary ladder is Conchona: "entre la diversidad de frutos menores, descollaba la formidable calabaza de su testa, con la gran boca de raja y dos ojuelos albinos, agujeros sin cristal, como practicados con un chuchillo" (*Luna*, p. 123). Don Cristobal's faithful servant Pepón has but a glimmer of animal intelligence: "donde yo he de estirar la pata... y tú... las cuatro patas" (*Bajo*, p. 219). The speechless Bermudo, Arias's constant companion, is less rational and humanly expressive than an animal; he is called "el mastín del príncipe" while Delfín, the real mastiff, plays the part of "trasgo" or "gnomo" (*La caída de los Limones*). The bestializing metaphor may become an ironic criticism of a whole class of men: "Bostezaba despaciosamente, ruidosamente, como un gran felino o un canónigo obeso" (*Tigre*, p. 21).

The narrator sometimes interrupts the portrayal of inner life to show a character's physical features, deformed into an infrahuman caricature: "de tarde en tarde se sonreía, enseñando unos dientes de blancura irreprochable, que, rodeados de hirsuto contorno, parecían una estría de carne de coco asomándose entre la cáscara pardusca y crinada" (*Belarmino*, p. 97). Although the dehumanizing vision is usually comic or demeaning, occasionally it reveals some positive but nonhuman quality. Even in praise, the author reifies his creatures.

> Parece que en lugar de piel tiene una ligera película, en amenazadora tirantez, como un globito de goma... que en lugar de estar inflado de hidrógeno lo estuviese de jovial humor sanguíneo. Es una alegría primaveral reprimida, a punto de agrietarse y supurar miel, o de hacer explosión; linda, fresca, sabrosa (*Ombligo*, p. 35).

People may appear as masked actors in a theatrical farce; facial features congeal into a stylized disguise that can be considered subjectively or objectively — the mask, not the man wearing it, causes pity or laughter: "Tigre Juan escuchó esta parrafada con su máscara verdosa de monstruo bufo, que así era espantosa como apiadable, y a ratos risible" (*Curandero*, p. 67). Don Sincerato's cough and laugh alternately mold his face into the traditional masks of comedy and tragedy: "Diferenciábase la risa, risa de calavera, de la tos, tos macabra, por el trazo que describía la cavidad de la boca, que en la tos era como carátula de tragedia y en la risa como máscara de farsa" (*Tigre*, p. 174). Such an image represents not only the objectifying vision of the author but also an extreme self-alienation in the character, whose personality breaks apart into a hidden, unexpressed self and an artificial social one. Don Sabas, the cynical politician of *Troteras y danzaderas*, wears a "carátula social" that has acquired an independent existence; his personality is concealed behind a fabricated semblance, a pasteboard replica that responds on its own to the theatrical conventions of society: "esa carátula social... que tiene vida propia, pero vida escénica" (p. 57).

While persons are deprived of humanity, objects are vivified, as if by contagion from the living beings with whom they are linked; once animated, they fuse with the latter to produce a strange, ambiguous hybrid. The forever frustrated, lascivious old man who spies on the serving maids of Congosto from the casino tower has become consubstantial with his telescope:

...adherido a su catalejo, en el cual parecía anhelar envasarse e inmiscuirse, como en el tubo de un embudo, y que había llegado casi a consubstanciarse con él, al modo de un apéndice orgánico, semejante a la trompa del oso hormiguero (*Ombligo*, p. 212).

In all these transformations the narrator caricatures physical appearance without referring to the feeling, thinking being behind it, a being made speechless in its debasement. But sometimes the body itself takes over the revelatory powers of language so that corporeal disturbances symbolize the silent inner self. Tigre Juan suffers from a total linguistic incapacity; he is so timid that either he fails to articulate sound ("Abrió la boca; una cavidad lóbrega, habitada por un silencio mortal... De la lengua se le desprendió, más que una palabra, un espectro de palabra", p. 68) or his words thoroughly distort his sentiments ("La melodía le resonaba cristalina y tácita dentro del cráneo, como lamento de ruiseñor... pero al sacarla a los labios degeneraba en graznido de palmípedo", p. 104). Invariably his behavior belies his intentions, for his expressive frustrations give others the impression of terrible ferocity.[2] Without the release of language, his spirit discloses itself only in physical spasms: "Tigre Juan no acertaba a articular la voz. Se puso verde. Bufaba. Estiraba y encogía el elástico pescuezo, rugoso y térreo como piel de paquidermo" (*Curandero*, p. 66).

Dissembling his omniscient knowledge, the author shows only meaningless surface detail. When this optical impressionism advances still further, it becomes expressionistic;[3] the narrator atomizes and personifies parts of the body and psychological states, and then recombines them in a grotesque assemblage of autonomous activities; man is depersonified while his physical features and thoughts are individually animated. Some descriptions recall Quevedo who shattered and reconstructed the human form in the same way (Pérez de Ayala alludes to his stylistic predecessor by

---

[2] "Todo aquello pretendía que fuesen chanzas graciosas y evidentes. Se esforzaba en susurrar palabras mimosas y dulcificar el acento; pero no le salían sino expresiones torvas y un rugido bronco" (*Tigre*, p. 23).

[3] Impressionism is the representation of sensory perception; one's knowledge of the object perceived is supressed in favor of unexplained surface details. In expressionism, the subject projects his emotions and attitudes onto external reality. See Charles Bally, Elise Richter, Amado Alonso, Raimundo Lida, *El impresionismo en el lenguaje* (Buenos Aires, 1943).

reworking the latter's famous "Érase un hombre a una nariz pegada" into "la temerosa e ingente nariz de Mur avanzaba por el claustro... trayendo en pos, casi escondido, al citado jesuita", *A. M. D. G.*, p. 221). The author substantializes emotions and perceptions, separating them from the percipient; [4] he exchanges sensory functions among different organs — the voice turns liquid, eyes become tactile:

> Su voz era un trémulo atenorado, de calidad oleaginosa, que se depositaba en el oído, gota a gota, como un beleno. A doña Mariquita le hacía el mismo efecto oírle que mirar su muestrario; sus palabras pulidas le producían impresión de abalorios, agremanes y cintas que le brotasen de la boca, como a un prestigitador de circo.
>
> La mirada de Vespasiano era táctil, como si del oscuro agujero de sus pupilas irradiasen elásticos y transparentes tentáculos de molusco, que iban a palpar el objeto con una caricia blanda. Las mujeres sentían que las desnudaba con aquellos brazos, traslúcidos, viscosos y cautos, que le salían de sus ojos (*Curandero*, p. 16).

Vespasiano is characterized by his effluvia: Herminia's attraction to him is pictured as the entanglement or glueing of her eyes in his lips: "quedaron adheridos, presos, en los labios brillantes y pegajosos de Vespasiano, como un ave atolondrada en la liga" (*Curandero*, p. 18). Eyes are also changed into mouths for drinking words and even the soul of another. In a concrete allegory of synaesthesia, not only do impressions merge and combine but the receptor organs themselves seem to be independently sensitive to inappropriate stimuli:

> Su mayor encanto consistía en los ojos, cuya forma y lineamento recordaban una boca de niño, con ambos párpados gordezuelos y color rosa, a manera de labios. Los entornaba que se dijera que escuchaba con ellos, como si bebiese las palabras y aun el alma, si miraban amorosos. (*Prometeo*, p. 170.)

---

[4] Doña Micaela's senses are autonomous and personified: "Casi, casi no tenía sentidos, puesto que no los utilizaba para entregarse al mundo ni deleitarse en su hermoso espectáculo, sino como espías y testigos de cargo, que traían noticias y delaciones desde fuera al interno tribunal de la inteligencia, la cual casi siempre dictaba fallos reprobatorios" (*Luna*, pp. 28-29).

Words, which for Pérez de Ayala are not only symbols but also real objects in their own right, easily assume material form. As the word is hypostatized the voice takes on the attributes of substance — color and fluidity: "Del rostro de plata lúcida que en la sombra albeaba, manó una hebra de plata, aprehensión de voz" (*Tigre*, pp. 85-6).

Ideas also materialize into visible entities: "No tenía ideas en la cabeza sino un enjambre de pequeñas sensaciones polícromas y zumbadoras" (*Troteras*, p. 152). Feelings and concepts may be represented as edible things absorbed and digested by another spirit, which is itself portrayed (in a figure of speech reminiscent of Unamuno) as a solid, fleshy thing: "Ingería con voluptuosidad los jugos más quintaesenciados, rancios y generosos del corazón e intelecto humano... y los asimilaba en sangre y carne de su espíritu" (*Prometeo*, p. 31).

Mechanized Action

The mechanization of action and the grouping of characters into a chorus or static frieze are both dehumanizing techniques; attention centers on movement that has become automatic and lifeless, either through the mindlessness of the actors or through the incomprehension of the spectator:

> Las mozucas volvían el tronco hacia adelante hasta casi dar con el rostro en las rodillas, y luego hacia atrás, como si fueran a caerse del asiento, levantando los brazos y desplomándolos de súbito desmayados y flojos; y repetían el juego una y otra vez, y muchas, como árboles endebles que agitase un huracán (*Tinieblas*, p. 95).

Secondary characters who augur the fate of the protagonist form a backdrop against which the latter must battle or before which he must perform. In *Luz de domingo*, the seven Becerril brothers are almost indistinguishable in appearance and in nastiness. Don Clemente's six daughters ("El profesor auxiliar") walk down the street in pairs, stepping lightly in a graceful, cadenced dance ("por no gastar el calzado"); they respond with identical gestures:

—¿No habéis oído?
Las cinco hermanas levantan la mano con que trabajaban, dejándola en suspenso; ladearon la cabeza; dejaron vagar la mirada y aguzaron el oído. Parecían cinco pájaros en un instante de sorpresa (*Ombligo*, p. 256).

The narrator synchronizes their actions and then segments the resultant single act into a series of photographic stills.

The fisher-women of the valley of Congosto are a dramatic chorus complete with tragic masks: "mujeres alharaquientas, como si de continuo educasen la garganta y la carátula para las imprecaciones ante la tormenta y el naufragio" (*Ombligo*, p. 20). In *Los trabajos de Urbano y Simona*, Simona's guardians, the seven spinster sisters, are fairy tale witches scarcely differentiated among themselves. Since their celibacy and *beatería* have made them monstrous, the author depicts them as vociferous gargoyles suspended from the house eaves: "Asomadas de cintura arriba, como siete gárgolas deformes, regurgitaban improperios en la noche callada" (p. 229).

In *Belarmino y Apolonio* the tragicomic scene in which Felicita shows her anxious concern for her ailing suitor is built on reiterated phrases and automatic gestures:

—¿Qué ruido es ése?— murmuró Felicita, incorporándose estremecida.—Parece que clavan un ataúd. Parece que cavan una fosa.

* * *

—¿Qué ruido es ése?— murmuró Felicita poniéndose en pie, transida de terror.—Parece que moscardonea un enjambre de espíritus. Parece que se oyen voces del otro mundo.

* * *

—¿Qué ruido es ése?— murmuró Felicita, cayendo de rodillas, desvariada.—Se oye murmurio de preces. Se oye chisporrotear de cirios. Rezan la recomendación de un alma. Anselmo ha muerto.

* * *

—¿Sueño? ¿Eres Tú? ¿Soy yo de carne? ¿No somos fantasmas? Telva respondía mentalmente; "¿Tú de carne? Puro hueso, y ya muy duro. ¿Pantasmas? No estás mala pantasmona..." (p. 135).

Felicita's anguished questioning about the reality of her existence is contaminated by literary formulae and clichés; she talks and acts like a mechanical puppet. The maid's sarcastic remarks, which shift the focus from Felicita's personal and tragic illusions to the spectacle of her corporeal ruin, also contribute to her depersonification.

Indirect Characterizations

Pérez de Ayala's characters are usually constructed on the armature of a moral attitude or ethical position. As incarnations of different theories about life and knowledge, most of them operate on a single motivational spring (or a single set of conflicting motives). This intentional simplification is particularly common among secondary characters who, because their author does not care to make them part of a life-like fictional world, are often more important as symbols than as actors in the drama (choral presentation is an example of this non-dynamic use of character). When he makes his protagonist equally uncomplicated, he seems to stabilize the disorder and mutability of reality into a system of neatly congruous paradigms. Instead of life-likeness, he aims at and achieves a completely abstract (inhuman) consistency.

The schematization of characters permits their portrayal in terms of contiguous elements that have nothing to do with their human qualities or with their behavior. Thus physiological peculiarities may express personality, as if the body were mirror of the soul, or a man's surroundings may manifest his nature so perfectly that he blends into them — the landscape or dwelling is personified while the man is reified. Such allusive, indirect presentation is a masking device,[5] for one or a number of purely external or

---

[5] In his *Theory of Literature* (Leningrad, 1931), Boris Tomaschevshij defines *mask* as a working out of concrete motifs harmonizing with the psychology of the character. Erich Auerbach, in *Mimesis* (Princeton, 1953) analyzes this technique in Balzac's descriptions; he observes that for the French writer, character and *milieu* are necessarily congruous (p. 417).

extraneous objective details signify an otherwise concealed subjectivity.

One "mask" that Pérez de Ayala fits onto almost every one of his personages is the emblematic name. Although generally only one item in a descriptive set that includes environment, mentality, and physical appearance, it sometimes anticipates all subsequent characterization, as in the case of the aging spinster, Felicita Quemada and of the fat, epicene, Anselmo Novillo. Occasionally, however, the name bears the descriptive burden by itself, summarizing everything that an outsider might know about the character, so that even when he later reveals his personality in deeds and words, the reader remains aware of a categorizing name-tag; examples are the ardent but chaste Cástulo Colera, the good-hearted priest, Sincerato Gamborena, and Telesoro Hurtado who absconds with the bank funds. Ironic designations reflect ambivalent judgements. Tigre Juan is sometimes called "don Juan" out of deference to his age; to those who claim that Apolonio Caramanzana's temperamental outbursts are nothing but histrionics calculated to hide the perfect equanimity of his soul, his name is entirely appropriate; yet his theatricality is as inconsonant with the apollonian ideal as is his chosen profession, which is, after all, under the patronage of Dionysius. The name may be a reversal of a character's traits, or it may be an ironic contrast to his fate, as with the timid Don Leoncio and his innocent, naive son Urbano (*Luna*) or the avaricious money-lender Ángel Bellido ("nombre propio como impropio"). Castor Cacigal (*Luz*), whose namesake is protector of sailors, dies at sea; Sor Resignación is "concisa y vehemente en sus requerimientos... precisamente del contraste del nombre y profesión con el temperamento de la monjita se engendraba la simpatía o encanto" (*Bajo*, 236); Marco de Setiñano's deformed, perverse son, Prometeo, is a perpetual onomastic reminder of the destruction of all his father's illusions.

The name may be the basis of a title pun (*La caída de los Limones*), or it may add a final irony to a story: in *Luz de domingo*, the early introduction of Doña Predestinación, the woman who runs the boarding house in which Castor lives, suggests the ineluctability of the young man's tragedy, but her marriage at the end of the novel to Deogracias Sánchez —making her Predestinación Sánchez, a common, ordinary fatality— seems to divest that tragedy of its heroic proportions and turn it into a poor, prosaic tale. In "El profesor auxiliar", the actors' names establish a comic allegory. Don Clemente, the timorous substitute professor is the butt of all the students' practical jokes. He has six daughters who create, by their names alone, the father's ironic situation: Clemencia, Caridad, Socorro, Esperanza, Olvido, and Piedad, are humble and home-bound, unable to aid or protect the teacher in the world. Ultimately, though, it is Don Clemente's Clemencia who saves him by intervening with one of the students. The story's plot is the elaboration of a word-play.

Most frequently the name is only one of a set of related characterizing masks. Don Cristóbal ("Padre e hijo") is as gigantic as his patron saint, but gigantic in every way ("Enorme, su valor; su osadía, enorme; enorme, su bondad; su amor y su odio, enormes; enorme su risa, y no menor su acento; su prodigalidad, enorme también" (*Bajo*, p. 221); his garden, "un jardin masculino, en el imperio de su fuerza espontánea" (p. 217), is an extensión of his being.⁶ His son Ignacio (a mocking reference to the Jesuits) is quite the reverse: weak-willed, womanish, vain, "de fofa gordura, como de eunuco". Angel Bellido is "por prestigio o metamorfosis la encarnación humana de aquella ictérica casuca de la Rúa Ruera, en donde el pintor Lirio calculaba que no podía vivir más que un prestamista" (*Belarmino*, p. 46).⁷ The feminine features of Vespasiano Cebón (Cebón = cepo + sebo) are the visible correlates of his essentially feminine nature; he does not pursue the female but is himself the object of attraction: "Era guapo, con una belleza de emperador romano o de señora madura en

---

⁶ On the other hand the monastery garden of "El otro padre Francisco" is metonymically described in terms of the protagonist's sensual nature: "Es... un parque pagano, afrodisíaco... los árboles indolentes rozan entre sí las ramas con suave temblor de voluptuosidad bucólica" (*Bajo*, p. 9). The garden of the convent where Belarmino believes Angustias is ımprisoned is the material projection of a mystical trance: "Asomaban los negros y rígidos cipreses, que eran como el prólogo del arrobo místico, el dechado de la voluntad eréctil y aspiración al trance; y los sauces anémicos y adolecientes... que eran fatiga y rendimiento, epílogo dulce del místico espasmo" (*Belarmino*, p. 142).

⁷ The house is personified to match its occupant: "En aquella casuca amarilla, de entrada abismática, como... boca desdentada, galería de vidrios como antiparras, y tejado redondo, negruzco y a trechos desguarnecido, como gorro mugriento, vive, sin duda, un prestamista" (*Belarmino*, p. 34).

libertinajes" (*Curandero*, p. 16), and his name is an emblem of this double comparison. His sexual ambiguity, which awakens "malsana curiosidad" in many women, is one aspect of that deficiency that impels him to create a personal legend; he exists truly only in the imagination of the women he must continually conquer.

In *Tigre Juan* and *El curandero de su honra*, physical and mental traits are so thoroughly amalgamated that all the characters have a look of artifice; these are not believable persons living in a real world but actors performing in rigidly prescribed roles. The design and precise detailing of the costumes and symbolic setting are more important than verisimilitude. For example, Doña Iluminada, viuda de Góngora, combines certain personality traits whose incompatibility is indicated in the chiaroscuro connotations of her name. Her first name and surname are doubly ambivalent because one cannot help but be reminded of the cliché about the "príncipe de luz, príncipe de tinieblas." The widow lives in a perpetual night in which the only "vislumbre de amanecer" is her absurd hope for the *curandero's* love (*Tigre*, p. 36); she is a composite of youth and withered old age that alternately dominate her appearance: "Su cándido rostro tenía, como el de la luna, crecientes y menguantes, plenitudes y ausencias, tan pronto emanaba un a modo de resplandor de plata como se hundía y borraba en el seno de la sombra" (p. 36). But her name is most significant in relation to her function in the novel: she can read the thoughts of others, penetrate their hidden selves with her luminous gaze ("ojos de lechuza adivinadora," p. 50; "pupila inquisidora y penetrativa," p. 76). A seer, to whom the future has been divinely revealed, she prophesies the unfolding of events and "illuminates" both Tigre Juan and Herminia as to the true cause of their own feelings. As sybil, she is often submerged in a hypnotic trance ("Doña Iluminada se me antoja que está sonámbula o en sueño cataléptico... A veces sale del trance con ojos pasmados," p. 37), and she seems to float midway between "el mundo de la materia y el del espíritu" (p. 72). The narrator alludes to this borderline existence by repeatedly speaking of her in terms of luminosity and obscurity:

> Desde el puesto se abarcaba el interior de la tienda, reducida y llena de fuliginosidad. Al fondo de la tienda... estaba la viuda, vestida de luto; la cara, blanca de papel; los

> ojos con una veladura de tristeza... Aun en las horas más altas del día, se escondía allí un manantial de tiniebla... Tigre Juan interpretaba este fenómeno como noche voluntaria, ordenada y presidida por la luna del cándido rostro de la dueña (*Tigre*, p. 30).

Whether she is concealing her own sentiments from Tigre Juan or enlightening Herminia about her unrecognized attraction to the *curandero*, the setting is painted in light and dark:

> Atardecía fuera. Dentro del tenducho se anticipaba la noche, y en medio, el óvalo nítido, casto, incorpóreo del rostro de doña Iluminada (p. 84).

> Este coloquio familiar se desarrollaba en la trastienda, anochecido, poco antes de la hora de la cena. Al volverse para salir, doña Marica dio de cara con la blanca y silenciosa viuda de Góngora (p. 228).

Her entrances are like moon-rises, luminous forecasts of the revelations she wants to impart. And her words, fittingly enough, bedazzle Herminia:

> Tiemblas como una alondra, hija mía. Mis razones se te figuran relumbres de espejuelo, que yo hago girar para traerte a la red donde caigas presa. Lo que yo... ando dando vueltas en la mano, es un puro diamante; el diamante de la verdad, y sus destellos... penetran y cruzan el cuarto oscuro de tu voluntad (p. 235).

The author has given a person a symbolic name and then exemplified its diverse connotations in descriptions and in the novel's plot. Iluminada's character emerges from a system of coordinated metaphors. [8]

---

[8] A last possible allusion might be that Doña Iluminada, like the *aluminados* or *iluminados* of the sixteenth-century, defends the directly revealed word of God, the divine law that frees one from the ties of conventional morality: "¡Ah, ya! La ley de los hombres. Pero hay, hija mía, otra ley, que es más santa: la ley de Dios. Y esa ley está en el corazón... Un segundo de felicidad compensa toda una vida de dolor" (*Curandero*, p. 42).

In an early story ("La Araña," 1913, in *La Revolución sentimental*), we find the germ of the theme of a clash between name and surname that is paralleled by a split in the personality:

> Se ve que el nombre y apellido de nuestro protagonista [Benigno Recio] conflagran entre sí, son dos elementos en pugna. De la

Externalization of Inner Reality

If minor figures frequently dissolve into their surroundings, the psychology of the protagonists is scarcely more substantial. Pérez de Ayala does not choose to depict inner life in such a way as to give the reader the impression of a direct, unmediated view of the mind. His active part in the creation must always be apparent. The narrative contrast between a subjective and an objective focus is more important than the subjectivity itself. When the characters' thoughts and feelings are necessary to the plot, they are not shown as they arise naturally, fragmented and disordered, but as mechanically arranged, observable phenomena.[9] For instance, passages in the free indirect style —a technique normally well adapted to the rambling flow of thought [10]— are repeatedly interrupted by explanations that draw the reader's attention back to the writer from whose pen the character is issuing.

And this indirect style often leads to a scenic device: the soliloquy, accompanied by stage directions for the action of the mind:

> Creyó ver primero una gran mancha roja, y luego un negror poblado de estrellitas rutilantes: "Aún bramas por la mujer, insensato, como ciervo sediento por el manantial... Señor de justicia, Señor de misericordia: ciégame." (*Tigre*, p. 73.)

(Tigre Juan, one of Pilares' most enthusiastic amateur actors, usually puts his interior monologues in the rhetorical phrasing he finds

---

propia suerte, en el carácter del hombre existía esta misma complejidad contradictoria, este continuo pendular desde la mansedumbre a la insolencia y desde la dulzura a la acritud (p. 58).

But the topic is limited to this paragraph and is not elaborated in the story's plot.

[9] Pérez de Ayala was certainly familiar with other technical possibilities for the representation of unconscious or barely conscious sentiments. In the Spanish novel alone, as early as 1884, Leopoldo Alas (in *La Regenta*) had developed extremely subtle ways of showing emotional or mental states and associations of which the character himself is not entirely aware.

[10] See Stephen Ullman, "Reported Speech and Internal Monologue in Flaubert" in *Style in the French Novel* (Cambridge, 1957) and Robert Humphrey, *Stream of Consciousness in the Modern Novel* (Berkeley and Los Angeles, 1958).

so effective before the public.) [11] The story "Justicia" opens with the soliloquy of a gypsy coppersmith in which the carefully balanced analogies in no way suggest the speaker's natural mode of expression:

> Señor soy del fuego. Pero el fuego señorea mis entrañas y me consume el alma.
> Señor soy del hierro. ¡Ay, corazón! Fueras pelota de hierro, salida de la fragua, y te forjaría con mi martillo pesado, seguro y frío.
> Señor soy del cobre. ¡Ay, pensamiento! Fueras hoja de cobre pulido y te repujaría a mi voluntad, en forma de copa, orlada de adormideras, para colmarla de olvido (*La revolución sentimental*, pp. 107-108).

This is a formal staged presentation. More obviously theatrical is the soliloquy matched with another in an unspoken dialogue like the silent exchange between Don Cástulo and Don Leoncio that closes the first scene of *Luna de miel, luna de hiel* or the mute duet between Tigre Juan and Herminia printed in parallel columns that begin with paired, identical sentences (*Curandero de su honra*).

To both indirect interior monologue and soliloquy, Pérez de Ayala prefers the author's description of consciousness, which he makes into a methodical analysis based on explanations of associated images and relevant information about the subject's past. The similes intended to clarify or illustrate the twists and turns of thought are logical and static; psychic life in these novels is not a fluid, multiform thing but an equilibrium of opposing forces ("por contrarrestar su atracción irresistible tenía que encastillarse en una proporcionada voluntad de repulsión", *Curandero*, pp. 44-45). Even when the state of mind depicted is chaotic, the character paradoxically organizes the inner turmoil into a coherent analogy:

---

[11] All of the soliloquies in this book are extremely formal. Doña Iluminada's speech is replete with aphorisims and word-plays; her logical and measured thought progresses by means of rational comparisons: "Pensaba, 'dos mañanas veo que tiran de mi vida. Cada mañana es un platillo de la balanza. Y mi vida en el fiel, temblando, como un niño asustado'" (*Tigre*, 82). Her imagery is as rhetorical as Tigre Juan's: "Oh, Desesperanza, compañera fiel de mis lástimas; perro que lame las llagas de su amo; tan encariñada estoy contigo que temo sanar, si he de perder tu compañía!" (p. 84).

> Al entrar, el depósito de granos, dispersos y confundidos sobre el tillado, se le presentó como imagen de su propia alma. Ideas y sentimientos hasta ahora clasificados y evaluados, rica cosecha de una larga experiencia, todo andaba ya, dentro de él, embrollado, mezclado, desperdigado. (*Tigre*, p. 140.)

Mental phenomena, we have noted, are imaginatively changed into palpable objects: "Estos pensamientos angustiosos giraban dentro del cráneo de Tigre Juan, afanándose en vano por salir a través de los ojos, como un moscardón que choca y vuelve a chocar contra el cristal de una ventana" (*Curandero*, p. 98). Lifting emotions, apprehensions, half-formed ideas out of the darkness of inner experience, the author hypostatizes them as autonomous figures playing in a farce observed by the passive part of the mind:

> No pudo conciliar el sueño. Revolvíase en su camastro humilde, zarandeada la imaginación a merced de un tumulto de pensamientos y emociones chocantes. Con premura y azoramiento se fugaba de una idea desagradable, volviéndole la espalda de la conciencia, e iba a tropezar con otra que igualmente le amedrentaba y repelía. Así en todas las direcciones del horizonte de la mente, como si hubiesen puesto asedio a su espíritu ansiedades y zozobras largo tiempo sumisas, amordazadas, y ahora rebeldes de pronto (*Tigre*, p. 70).

The climactic scene of *Tigre Juan* is another spectacle in which the *dramatis personae* are feelings and memories.

Pérez de Ayala, obviously not concerned with an illusionistic picture of inner reality, objectifies the stream of consciousness, congeals it into a concrete, perceptible substance that serves as a visible foil to the action: the outer charade of speech and movement is complemented by the inner charade of thought.

Structural Framing

The novel as a self-contained imaginary orb in which verisimilitude is achieved by carefully preventing any intrusion from the outer, non-literary world, is not the model for the ironic novelist. Such a writer deliberately weakens the illusion of reality by destroying what Ortega called the novel's "closed precint." [12] He calls attention to the work's fictitiousness. Insisting that events and characters, which might seem convincing within their own realm, are, after all, the products of his devising, the narrator turns life into art, into a story, legend, or apologue. Detached esthetic perspective replaces that of personal human involvement. In emphasizing his own creative role, Pérez de Ayala shows how the novelist can arbitrarily change the boundaries of the real and the fictitious: he makes the reader a witness to the emergence of literary dramas from the world of ordinary, every-day happenings. Reality and fiction contaminate each other. Artistic transpositions are one means of shifting the focus on the narrative subject; another, related technique is to frame the story with extraneous materials so that its structural supports become conspicuous. Pérez de Ayala uses several framing devices. He may set the fiction between introductory and closing essays in which he addresses the reader directly, or he may situate the main plot within another that is incidental to it. The narrator sometimes emphasizes the time gap between the story's events and his own present, or he suspends the action with digressive comments and observations. In all of these cases, the switch is from a subjective or sympathetic view to an aloofly objective one, from the illusion of real life to obvious literary form.

In Pérez de Ayala's first novel, *Tinieblas en las cumbres* (1907) a rudimentary framing technique is combined with a dual perspective on a single incident, a combination that anticipates the composition of *Belarmino y Apolonio*. The novel begins with a preface that parodies the *pícaro's* traditional justification for the recitation of his sins; the narrator further delays his story with a *Prolegómenos* in which, with satirically erudite style replete with Latin and Greek quotations, he discourses on the history of prostitution; a third and final digression is an anecdote involving one of the minor characters. The action does not start until the

---

[12] Hace falta que el autor sepa primero atraernos al ámbito cerrado que es su novela y luego cortarnos toda retirada, mantenernos en perfecto aislamiento del espacio real que hemos dejado... Es menester que el autor construya un recinto hermético, sin agujero ni rendija por los cuales, desde dentro de la novela, entreveamos el horizonte de la realidad (Ortega y Gasset, *op. cit.*, 410-411).

fourth chapter of Part I. The scene is a Pilares brothel and the point of view is that of a third-person narrator who reports the words and gestures of people without entering into the consciousness of any of them. The whole of Part II is an intercalated biography of one of the prostitutes, Rosina, told this time by an omniscient author who describes her thoughts and sentiments. Concluding this episode is a repetition of the closing scene of Part II, but whereas it was then presented objectively, it is now recorded through the emotional reactions of Rosina. Because this biographical interlude does not appear in a flashback, as a memory in the mind of one of the characters in the main story, it stands apart as a distinct approach to a certain episode; it provides the interior perspective of a secondary personage.

The early story "Exodo" is constructed on three levels of increasing subjectivity. It opens with a stage-like scene in which several *salladores* pause in their work to watch the feudal lord ride over a distant hill to the hunt; their remarks are cast in playformat that, together with the archaic dialect and the references to Galaico-Asturian superstitions, evoke not so much a real man as a hero of popular legend: Don Cristóbal is derealized by the creation of his own local myth.[13] The peasants' view of him is remote, both physically and humanly. But in the second section the observation point is closer, within the old manor-house kitchen where an ancient nurse comforts Don Cristóbal's child while upstairs the lord and his retainers celebrate drunkenly. Again the artifice of stage dialogue maintains a rather abstract quality. Paradoxically, these two theatrically composed sections do not make the action more dramatic or more immediate; they are static illustrative passages that define the hero but do not advance the action. The protagonist enters his tale indirectly, reflected first in mirrors placed far and near. The third and last section contains the whole

---

[13] *El señor Ruperto, de Las Llosas*
   Nada nin naide le mete susto.
....
Selva, la Roxa
   Non cura de les ánimes.
Pedrín, de Manuela
   Nin de la huestia.
Nolo, de Pedrosa
   Nin de los difuntos
El señor Restituto Remirao
   Nin de la Iglesia y Jesucristo ("Éxodo," *Bajo*, p. 174).

of the plot — Don Cristóbal's ridiculous and barbaric act (the burning of his mansion and estate to rid them of a plague of fleas). The incongruity between the stylized introductory scenes (which make up two thirds of the story) and the absurd denouement gives the work the character of an *esperpento*, a fiction deformed by a comic-grotesque vision.[14]

"Clib" (*El ombligo del mundo*) is an apologue whose moral is embodied in the narrative structure. The introduction, told in the first person, reports a conversation between the narrator and a friend about certain psychological and social theories which are then illustrated in the tale that follows, told now not by the actor-narrator of the opening, but by a third-person omniscient author; the story closes with the conversation of the opening part. The protagonist's death occurs in both accounts, but although it is a peripheral incident in the frame narration, it is the climax of the inner story. Pérez de Ayala has designed the two-layered narrative in such a way that schematic shifts in point of view accompany the alternations between general principle and particular example.

Sometimes the author severs the ties between fiction and the contemporary world by placing the story in an unchanging past, surrounding it with a moat of time. He begins "El profesor auxiliar" with a specific reference to a temporal gap and an action scene in chorus that, like those of "Exodo," frames the plot by retarding its commencement. At the conclusion, the author returns to his position in the present, from the vantage point of which Don Clemente's entire history appears irrevocable and fatally determined.

In the "poematic" novel *Prometeo*, the structural display of theme becomes even more evident. This is a thesis novel that admonishes against prideful attempts to subjugate life to the systems of reason, (a thesis directly stated in some of the introductory poems); but the message is included within a broader, not so precisely defined theme (reality's multiple facets) which is expressed through manipulations of tone and point of view and through alternations between a direct and a "literary" presentation. The

---

[14] Valle-Inclán's first two "comedias bárbaras," *Aguila de blasón* (1907) and *Romance de lobos* (1908) antedate this story which was written in 1910.

novel opens with a series of prefaces in mock-epic style that not only put off the beginning of the story but also give it an artificial, parodic quality. The narrator, addressing himself to the reader, laments the decline of the epic, the degeneration of heroic song into mere novel. Then, having apologized for his digressions, he summarizes the adventures of his modern Odysseus in pseudo-epic phrasing, indicating in his tone the complete estrangement of the ironic spectator. In Chapters II and III, which retell and translate into modern prose the summary in Chapter I, and in the continuation of the plot in Chapter IV, the author brings the myth down to the level of everyday reality; the comic burlesque of Marco de Setiñano's unheroic life is replaced by the more personal version of an omniscient narrator who can depict the mental processes as well as the acts of his characters. In Chapter V, the perspective structure is again altered: a more limited and objective narrator gives an account of the short and unhappy life of Marco's feeble and perverse son, Prometeo. Although Prometeo's tragedy is part of his father's, since it represents the ironic reversal of the latter's aspirations, the author no longer describes Marco's consciousness, nor even Prometeo's: he has suddenly restricted his omniscience to the world of speech and action. This story, almost an epilogue to Marco de Setiñano's, is laconic and devoid of emotional coloring; it is a chronicle of facts rather than an analysis of human motives and sentiments. Significantly it ends, not with the boy's last act, his suicide, but with a graphic picture of the corpse ("bailaba al aire el cuerpo de Prometeo, deforme y liviano como fruto serondo," p. 82). The initial comic detachment is reflected in the concluding objective detachment. Exemplifying the theme of disparate human realities, the author has successively regarded a person's life as comedy, tragedy and objectively observed phenomenon.[15]

---

[15] At the end of *El curandero de su honra*, the author attaches a *Parergón*, made up of conversations between the principal characters that supposedly take place during the period of time summarized in the *Coda*; it closes with a scene between Tigre Juan and Vespasiano that brings the theme of their complementary natures to its logical conclusion ("Eres una parte de mí mismo, que me falta; como yo debiera ser una parte de ti," p. 151). Since the material might seem superfluous to the ordinary reader, the narrator claims to have included it for the sake of "el lector exigente y curioso de la historia interna" (p. 124). The dialogues are brief

THE SHIFTING PERSPECTIVE OF THE NARRATOR   43

It is in the short novel *La caída de los Limones,* that Pérez de Ayala most thoroughly exploits the frame technique in elaborating his relativistic theme. The basis of the plot (an actual occurrence) is a violent crime whose antecedents and consequences serve as the material for an exercise in contrasting perspectives.

The story of the Limón family of Guadalfranco is framed by an account of events in a Madrid *pensión.* The first two chapters and the concluding one are told in the first person by a witness to what happens in the boarding house where the two Limón sisters are staying. The narrator does not (cannot) reveal the identity of these two women; instead he describes his own curiosity about them.[16] The reader first learns about the Limón family through someone who was a stranger to its tragedy, someone who is, furthermore, separated from it by an undefined period of time (as in most first person accounts, the narrator is looking back upon scenes from the past).

The story itself does not begin until Chapter III when another narrator, this time an omniscient one, summarizes the circumstances that led to the central action. Both the setting and the time level are different from those of the first two chapters; the action takes place in the ancient provincial city of Guadalfranco, some time previous to the Madrid incidents. Thus the main action is not introduced through a flashback or remembrance on the part of one of the characters, but as a separate and independent narration. The archaic style and unusual syntax of the first few pages make this locale seem quite remote from the prosaic, contemporary world of the Madrid boarding house. Indeed, Gudalfranco, sunken

---

disquisitions on two topics previously developed in the novel, free will and the relativity of truth; one new subject is introduced in a debate between Tigre Juan and Colás: the conflict between life's "sinrazón" and generic, undeviating reason. The *Parergón* is not exactly part of a frame (a last look at the people and events from an objective viewpoint) because the colloquies are simply a more complete exposition of opinions already aired; no new perspective on either action or ideas is offered. The author's description of this section is accurate—"un documento accesorio."

[16] The double refraction of all objects of focus in this novel begins with a stylistic bifurcation: the narrator describes the physical appearance of the two women, first with delicacy, then in the harsh terms of vulgar opinion: "Eran humildemente dolorosas. Su dolor, cualquiera que fuese la causa, sugería la idea de un destino mujeril malogrado, algo así como la tristeza de la virginidad vetusta. O como se dice en el duro lenguaje de cada día, tenían toda la traza de ser dos solteronas" (p. 154).

into a soporific and almost imaginary existence, is so unknown and unreal to the rest of Spain that many people think it is a political fabrication, a town invented by Sagasta to provide jobs and patronage incomes. The narrator surveys the parallel declines of the city and the house of Uceda and tells of the marriage between the last Uceda and Enrique Limón, an ambitious and successful *cacique*. The poem prefacing Chapter IV introduces still another perspective, that of the fairy tale: "El príncipe lindo pasea el jardín. / Al diestro, la reina, con gran capirote. / Detrás la nodriza conduce el mastín /.../ El señor Jilguero, trovero laureado / canta mil lisonjas al príncipe real: / El mundo es un vasto país encantado" (*Prometeo*, p. 172). The prose narrative, which consists only of the author's summary and in which the actors have not yet begun to move or talk, does not break the timeless, magical silence of the setting. We enter a real human drama, which strangely enough will take place in an apparently mythical city, through the anteroom of fantasy. In Chapters V and VI the figures are animated, endowed with speech and mobility. The story develops (as do most omniscient author narrations) in a fictive or dramatic present; the verb tenses are, of course, past, but since there is no reference to a later vantage point from which the action is viewed, it seems to be unfolding now; the reader locates the present in the forward movement of the plot. Chapters VII and VIII present the principal dramatic motifs: the lust for power of Enrique Limón and his eldest daughter, Fernanda, and the jealousy that Domenica Limón's love for Próspero Merlo awakens in her brother Arias. Chapter VII is almost entirely scene with dialogue, but in VIII the narrator increases the depth of his omniscience when he reveals (though in summary manner, for the pace of this short novel is rapid) the unspoken sentiments of Domenica, Arias, and Bermudo. Arias's incestuous love for Domenica, the underlying cause of his crime, is not developed beyond the bare indication needed for the motivation of the action. Because the author is not here concerned with psychological phenomena for their own sake but only as determinants of plot, he presents inner life through its outward dramatic form instead of through lengthy subjective analyses. Tracing the dynamic trajectory of an unavoidable tragedy rather than its source in character or its effects thereon, he makes the theme emerge from the plot structure itself. The *shift* from the external account of words and gestures to the inward scene is more important than the psychology of the person described. The relativity of any human situation is represented by contraposing different perspectives; the technique is more theatrical than novelistic and suggests the outward form of the drama, the spectacle. It is only one more step to the presentation of spectacle devoid of meaning. Arias's suffering is incomprehensible to his dull-witted, faithful servant Bermudo who "no acierta a comprender la tramoya del dramático tinglado". Life is its staged version.

In Chapter IX the narrator temporarily abandons the fictive present to adopt a retrospective attitude towards what is really the novel's climax; he evades the direct presentation of the crime, the rape of the daughter of the widow Candelero and the murder of both women, and gives instead a succint review of the incident that reads much like a police bulletin with its dry listing of evidence, suspicion, etc. The author has narrowed his omniscience again, reporting only the characters' words and withholding from the reader the knowledge of Arias's guilt. Chapter X, in which Arias confesses to Domenica, consists almost entirely of dialogue; we are given no clue to the thoughts of brother and sister and at the end of the chapter even speech is eliminated in favor of a terse summary of acts ("Al conocer la sentencia, Fernanda y Domenica fueron a la carcel a ver a su hermano por última vez y luego se ausentaron de Guadalfranco", p. 224) The chronicler who opened Chapter II and who has shown parts of the drama at close range has now concluded.

The scene of Chapter XI is the Madrid boarding house, and the story is taken up again by the narrator-observer who tries to interpret what he sees, but who has no access to the minds of others. He tells about his own reaction to the newspaper account of Arias and Bermudo's execution instead of dramatically picturing its effect on the Limón sisters. And as if to provide a still more alien perspective on the tragedy, the novel ends with the jeering remarks of another boarder in the *pensión*, a man who considers the hanging in the inhuman terms of political expediency. "Les está bien merecido. Esto es lo que hay que hacer con todos los caciques" (p. 232).

The author first views externally one chance episode in a human drama; then, assuming partial omniscience, he relates past events, and finally, with total knowledge of his characters, he discloses their inner selves. When he arrives at the crime on which the tragedy turns, he reverses the procedure until he is once again an outside observer. Coordinated with these changes in perspective are changes in time and setting. As the narrator closes in on the real-life drama of Arias and Domenica, the scene switches from the indubitable reality of the Madrid *pensión* to a vague, half-legendary feudal city where we come upon the private fairy-tale world of Domenica and Arias. If in the solid and mundane Madrid the Limón story is nothing but an item of juridical information, in the almost imaginary Gaudalfranco, it is a real tragedy suffered by real persons. The reality of setting is in inverse relation to the immediacy of the drama.

The author suggests still other perspectives in the historian's archaic style in Chapter III, in the interpolated fairy tale of Chapter IV, and in the introductory poems that are symbolic versions of the story, allegorical keys to the text that situate the fall of the Limóns in a universal scheme of eternal antagonisms, birth/death, good/evil, etc.[17] This allusion to a universal design, to the ultimate conciliation of opposites, establishes the most remote perspective of all, that of the artist who sees painful reality as "un juego de bellas fuerzas naturales".

Symmetrical Plots and their Concrete Representation

In the same way that Pérez de Ayala objectifies the inner life of his characters, he projects his own bifurcating vision outwards, creating antithetical human types and composing his narrative on the basis of symmetrically balanced parts. He may present the antagonists in a novel as the severed halves of a single unit, each complementing and fulfilling the other: Tigre Juan claims that Vespasiano, his rival in love, is his ideal half ("le amaba como su otra mitad ideal; el otro yo, que él hubiera preferido ser", *Curandero*, p. 27); Belarmino and Apolonio, whose life histories are

---

[17] "Tan-tan. Tan-tan. / Las campanas en los campanarios / anuncian al caballero blanco. / ¡Oh luminoso arcano! Tan-tan. Tan-tan. / Las campanas en los cementerios / anuncian al caballero negro. / ¡Oh sombrío misterio!" (p. 225).

almost identical, are like reversed mirror images, and they themselves recognize the underlying unity of this opposition when, after years of enmity, they are reconciled ("Eres como mi otra mitad. Sí, y tú mi otro testaferro", *Belarmino*, 187). The central situation of a novel is often grotesquely or comically reflected among the minor characters: in *Belarmino y Apolonio* the love of Angustias and Pedro is set off against the absurd and impossible love of Felicita Quemada and Pedro Novillo; in *Luna de miel, luna de hiel*, the amorous awakening of Urbano and Simona is paralled in the comic romance of Don Cástulo and Conchona. In *Tigre Juan* and *Curandero de su honra* the love story of the *curandero* and Herminia contrasts with the frustration of Doña Iluminada and the emotional aridness of Vespasiano, and the last two characters are paired as opposite types of sterility.[18] Duplicating situations are paralleled by duplications in the action: Doña Iluminada engineers both the love affairs of Tigre Juan and Herminia and of Colás and Carmina, and the motif of love fostered by a third person appears again in the intercalated story of Carmen and Lino, with Herminia as intermediary. The plot may split into diverging trajectories (creating a pattern similar to the "hour-glass" one observed by E. M. Forster in Anatole France's *Thaïs*); the young Urbano's sudden revulsion toward sexual love occurs just as his mother, on the verge of old age, for the first time feels desire for her husband, a desire grotesquely underscored by her precipitate physical decline which is, in turn, matched by the equally sudden and horrible aging of Don Leoncio's mistress; concurrent reversals are paired in an improbable and farcical equilibrium.[19]

The symmetry of *Tigre Juan* is not limited to the unfolding of the love stories; the unifying theme, the passage from

---

[18] "Doña Iluminada era la esterilidad desengañada y resignada, que no siendo de provecho para sí resuelve emplear su energía inútil en beneficio ajeno. Vespasiano era la esterilidad insumisa, que se engaña a sí propia" (*Curandero*, p. 13).

[19] "Micaela enflaquecía rápidamente — y era ya flaca —; María Egipcíaca engordaba por instantes — y cuidado que era mantecosa...— La piel de doña Micaela ennegrecía. La de María Egipcíaca no cedía en blancura a la cal de las paredes. Las manos de doña Micaela eran sarmentosas y ardían; las de María Egipcíaca, gordezuelas, muelles, frías y húmedas. En lo que entrambas se identificaban era en la pasión, contenida y celada en la una, desbordada en la otra" (*Trabajos*, pp. 143-44).

incomprehension to understanding, is pictured throughout the novel by a set of concrete symbols. Concepts are thus displayed in sensory images and exemplified in certain significant situations. For example, all of the characters are blind to reality, either because of a stubborn refusal to deal with it or because of some kind of obfuscating delusion; Don Sincerato's asylum for blind deaf-mutes is a miniature model of the whole of the novel's world. *Tigre Juan* ends with the old priest's lamentation on human blindness and the impossibility of true communication,[20] and the next volume (*Curandero*) begins with the same topic when, at the wedding of Tigre Juan and Herminia, Sincerato's pupils perform in sign language a "mute and cabalistic" song about the illusion of the senses and the deceits of the spoken word; truth is both invisible and silent. The objectification of the various connotations of Iluminada de Góngora's name and the plays on words in the discovery scenes in both volumes are also graphic representations of ideas and action. The psychological drama is externalized by using certain figures of speech in a purely literal sense. Thus, "illumination" and "enlightenment," synonyms for rational comprehension, are made to refer to perceptible light, so that the play of light and dark in the descriptive passages becomes a visual accompaniment to the mental phenomena for which the terms were originally devised. Pérez de Ayala resuscitates "dead" metaphors to illustrate the action.

A system of images at once derived from the plot and picturing it, establishes two levels within the work: on one the characters act and on the other the author unfolds a graphic allegory. The second level implies a detached, esthetic perspective—it is as if the narrator were showing at the same time reality and its representation. In subjecting incidents to an obvious symmetry and in interweaving ideas and their respective images, Pérez de Ayala makes his own presence felt: the point of view that regards the dramatic action as if it were real is always complemented by that of the artist who is creating.

---

[20] "¡Pobres hombres y mujeres! Ojos tienen y no ven; oídos, y no oyen; boca, y no atinan a expresar lo que quieren. ¡Señor, Señor!... Atended, locos. Los que llamáis ciegos son los que mejor ven, porque no han menester luz; sordos y mudos, los que mejor hablan, porque para ellos el silencio es elocuente'" (*Tigre*, p. 247).

Chapter II

THE MULTIPLE PERSPECTIVES OF THE CHARACTERS. BELARMINO Y APOLONIO

The narrator shifts his attention from the internal to the external, from psychological content to either pure corporeity or esthetic form. But perspectivism can also be represented within the novel by endowing each character with a distinct point of view; a multifaceted fly-like retina replaces the stereoscopic focus of the narrator, who now pretends that his is just one of many possible interpretations. Confronting a world they find puzzling and contradictory, the characters express a variety of opinions, see and describe each other in terms of private sets of values, so that each event considered by them fractures into several realities. Tying together all the discrepant views and implicitly judging all the conflicting theories is the ironic author, who provides, in his humor, the most relativistic note of all.

The most obvious example of prismatic vision is the simple enumeration of contrary explanations, completed perhaps, by a comment on the inadequacy of all of them:

> En Regium se sustentaban diferentes hipótesis acerca de Gonzalfañes. Quiénes aseguraban que era demente..., cuáles que sufría de infortunios amorosos... Éstos, que las complicaciones de cierto horroroso atentado le mantenían recoleto en su fortaleza agreste. Aquéllos, que era un idiota, atacado de misantropía. Lo cierto es que ninguno sabía nada (*A. M. D. G.*, pp. 11-12).

The narrator himself may summarize the possibilities: "Padre Siquieros ha enmagrecido y perdido la turgencia juvenil del rostro, bien a causa de una enfermedad, acaso por obra de morales sufrimientos, quizá en virtud de penitencias excesivas; tal vez por las tres cosas juntamente" (*A. M. D. G.*, p. 32). The survey of different interpretations is sometimes a way of withholding knowledge. At the beginning of *Tigre Juan*, the market place idlers, who have not been able to find out much about the *curandero*, speculate about his mysterious past: "Decíase que era viudo y que había asesinado a su primera mujer; quiénes se aseguraban por hartazgo de matrimonio; otros que como sanción de una ofensa al honor conyugal" (p. 21). The narrator does not tell the protagonist's history but teases the reader with the uncertainties of local gossip. Frequently an incident is duplicated in two different accounts. The degree of involvement in the action changes with the narrative focus, which may be that of a witness or an omniscient author. We have noted the repetition of scenes in his first novel, *Tinieblas en las cumbres*, in "Clib," *Prometeo*, and *La caída de los Limones*. *A. M. D. G.* includes a mosaic of perspectives; the action is reported not only in the author's narration but also through stage-like dialogue scenes and through excerpts from the writings of two of the characters (Padre Olano's marginal notes and directions for his retreat sermons and pages from Bertuco's diary). In *Troteras y danzaderas* a single scene is split into five distinct points of view: "*Punto de vista de don Sabas...*; *Punto de vista de Rosina...*", etc. (p. 72). But in *Belarmino y Apolonio*, Pérez de Ayala's relativism becomes the primary configurative theme, providing the subject matter, informing the style, and determining the carefully contrived structure of the novel.

Belarmino y Apolonio

Before commenting on the novel's composition, a brief summary of its plot will be useful. In the Prologue ("El filósofo de las casas de huéspedes"), the author tells about a boarding house companion he knew many years ago, Don Amaranto de Fraile; this man's ideas on knowledge, drama, and philosophy take up most of the section. Chapter I ("Don Guillén y la Pinta") introduces two other people he had met in Madrid at another time, a priest, Don Guillén Caramanzana and a prostitute called "la

Pinta." They tell him about their fathers, Apolonio Caramanzana, a shoemaker-dramatist, and Belarmino Pinto, a shoemaker-philosopher. In Chapter II ("Rúa Ruera, vista desde dos lados"), the narrator starts out to describe the street in Pilares where the two shoemakers lived, but then digresses into a discussion of novelistic technique. Belarmino's story begins in Chapter III ("Belarmino y su hija"). Chapter IV ("Apolonio y su hijo") consists almost entirely of Don Guillén's recitation of his personal history. Chapter V ("El filósofo y el dramaturgo") switches back to the two shoemakers and the intellectual rivalry that existed between them. Chapter VI ("El drama y la filosofía") tells what happens to them after the unexpected elopement and subsequent separation of their children, Angustias and the seminary student, Pedrito. In Chapter VII ("Pedrito y Angustias"), Don Guillén gives his version of the episode and reviews his life from then to the present; the narrator now enters the story and reunites the long-parted lovers (Pedro and Angustias, alias, Don Guillén and "la Pinta"). The last chapter (Chapter VIII, "Sub specie aeterni") returns to the shoemakers who hear about the young people's reunion and at last end their long feud. In the Epilogue, the author gives an account of some posthumous papers left by Don Froilán Escobar, one of Belarmino's disciples. An appendix lists a sampling of Belarmino's private vocabulary.

Theoretical Perspectives

The author introduces the central theme of his novel — the relativity of knowledge — through the speculations of a minor character, Don Amaranto de Fraile. In the Prologue the narrator recalls this person's distrust of the sciences and his belief that only through drama and philosophy can one understand human life. Amaranto's conceptions of these "disciplines" are counterbalanced and contradicted in the Epilogue by the views of another minor character, Froilán Escobar. The former asserts that whereas drama penetrates man's inner being, philosophy considers his acts in the light of eternal categories (*sub specie aeterni*); the two approaches, are, nevertheless, inseparable, for philosophical contemplation inevitably follows dramatic empathy. Escobar, on the other hand, maintains that the dramatist, far from delving into the tragedy of his fellow men and sharing their sufferings, only simulates emotion: "Hay una paradoja del dramaturgo; es la misma que Diderot llamó paradoja del comediante. La emoción no se comunica sino que se provoca. Para provocar una emoción hay que mantenerse frío... [El dramaturgo] finge ser actor siempre; y siempre es espectador, espectador de sí mismo" (p. 191). The philosopher is the one who immerses himself in all dramas: "Por de fuera, serenidad, impasibilidad; en lo más secreto, ardor inextinguible... El filósofo vive todos los dramas; jamás es espectador" (p. 192).

This disagreement between the two men is proof of the relativity of truth: "Tan verdad puede ser lo de don Amaranto como lo de Escobar; y entre la verdad de Escobar y la de don Amaranto se extiende un sinnúmero infinito de otras verdades intermedias, que es lo que los matemáticos llaman el *ultracontinuo*. Hay tantas verdades irreductibles como puntos de vista" (p. 193). Since all theories grasp some part of reality, one can faithfully represent it only by showing as many views of a thing as possible. Such a composite picture can be schematically suggested by choosing from the continuum of possible perspectives any two diametrically opposed points: "Yo he querido presentar, acerca de Belarmino y Apolonio, los puntos de vista de don Amaranto, y de Escobar, porque entre ellos cabe inscribir todos los demás, ya que por ser los más antitéticos, son los más comprensivos" (*loc. cit.*). The ideas of Amaranto and Escobar exemplify in their antithesis the relativity of knowledge; standing like reflecting mirrors at the beginning and end of the novel, they serve as both the structural and conceptual frames.

In the second chapter the author applies the principle of contrasting views to the problems of writing fiction. Again Don Amaranto is spokesman for the dual approach: in an imaginary dialogue with the narrator, he advises him to refrain from giving his own description of the story's setting, the Rúa Ruera of Pilares. He warns the author about the difficulties of showing a complicated, many-layered reality through the two-dimensional projection of fiction. The linear and chronological ordering of events simplifies and distorts experience. Although each person and each act is a cluster of different points of view, the novelist traditionally presents only his own cycloptic vision, thereby reducing the action to a single plane surface and a single temporal succession:

> Describir es como ver con un ojo, paseándolo por la superficie de un plano, porque las imágenes son sucesivas en el tiempo, y no se funden, ni superponen, ni, por lo tanto, adquieren profundidad. En cambio, la visión propia del hombre, que es la visión diafenomenal, como quiera que, por enfocar el objeto con cada ojo desde un lado, lo penetra en ángulo y recibe dos imágenes laterales que se confunden en una imagen central, es una visión en profundidad. El novelista, en cuanto hombre, ve las cosas estereoscópicamente, en profundidad; pero, en cuanto artista, está desprovisto de medios con que reproducir su visión. No puede pintar; únicamente puede descubrir, enumera (p. 28).

Amaranto's advice for correcting this defective vision is to cleave the narrative focus in two: "Busca la visión diafenomenal. Inhíbete en tu persona de novelista. Haz que otras dos personas la vean al propio tiempo, desde ángulos laterales contrapuestos" (p. 29). Just as the theorist can represent the infinity of truth by pairing any two antithetical ideas, the novelist can evoke the many-sidedness of experience by filtering his material through duplicating but reverse points of view.[1] By way of immediate and specific example, the author draws from memory two characters, Lirio, a painter, and Lario, a positivist, and lets his recollection of

---

[1] Don Amaranto compares the novelist and the painter, observing that the latter is able to dominate his subject through the use of perspective (28). Leon Livingstone, in "Interior Duplication and the Problem of Form in the Modern Spanish Novel," *PMLA,* LXXIII (1958), 404, interprets this comparison too literally when he says that "in thus making incessant demands on himself for the achievement of vision in depth, the novelist will have inevitable recourse to the techniques which most readily permit this effect, notably painting—with its natural depth of perspective—and music—with the cumulative profundity of its contrapuntal treatment." But Amaranto's "pintar" is only a metaphor for the literary presentation of a many-layered reality. Perspective in painting has nothing to do with perspective in the novel; the first is a method for creating an illusion of deep space (a visual technique), and the second is a method for suggesting the subjective/objective poles of experience (a dramatic technique). Amaranto's statement that the artist has no means of reproducing his humanly diaphenomenal vision should not be taken as an expression of the author's opinion, for Pérez de Ayala demonstrates quite the contary throughout the novel.

their argument about the Rúa Ruera stand in place of his own picture. Using the device of a double focus, Pérez de Ayala composes the whole novel as a counterpoint of perspectives. He even goes so far as to deny having a point of view of his own: "Y singularmente he apelado a la ciencia y doctrina de estos caballeros, por disimular que frente a Belarmino y Apolonio, ni tenía ni tengo punto de vista determinado" (p. 193).

As if to support this last statement, the author incorporates into his fiction the philosophical and dramatic theories of both Amaranto and Escobar. Amaranto's ideas are evident in the arrangement of the chapters, which is determined not by chronology but by the movement from a sympathetic presentation — the central part of the book — to an abstract consideration of conflict and harmony — the last chapter, titled *Sub specie aeterni*. And Escobar's characterizations of the dramatist and the philosopher are embodied in Apolonio and Belarmino: the first is the perennially unmoved dramatist who takes advantage of life's calamities in order to show off his mimetic skill ("Apolonio se sentía orgullosísimo, creyéndose en aquellos momentos un personaje trágico de verdad e imaginando inspirar a la duquesa fuerte interés patético", 119), while Belarmino, the philosopher, is so devoted to his own subjectivity that when tragedy comes upon him, he solipsistically denies the external world ("Fuera de uno mismo —pensaba Belarmino— no existía nada. El mundo era una ilusión de los sentidos, un espejismo de la imaginación. El mundo de fuera era creación aparente y engañosa del mundo de dentro", 143). Thus the hypotheses that frame the novel are also elaborated within it. Indeed, the principle of the double view is illustrated not only by the polarities of Amaranto and Escobar's thought but also by the very combination of "theory" and "fact": we move from general ideas on drama and philosophy to the concrete examples of a "philosopher" and a "dramatist," from speculation to life and then back again (thus demonstrating Amaranto's contention that the generalizing and particularizing approaches are inseparable). The logical view encloses the aesthetic: the characters are considered "philosophically" in the Prologue and Epilogue, "dramatically" in the intervening chapters. So thoroughly are the novel's generative ideas fused with its total pattern that theme and form, theory and expression, are indistinguishable.

Structural Perspectives

The story is told from three separate points of view; each narrator, selecting different details and coloring them with his own feelings, gives a slightly different account. The two principal perspectives belong to the author who undergoes a strange miosis and splits into an omniscient author and a first person narrator-witness; whereas the first describes everything that happens, whether in the characters' minds or in the outer realm of speech and action, the second, unable to read the thoughts of the people he observes, writes down only what he sees and hears. The third perspective is that of one of the characters, Don Guillén, who tells his story to the narrator-witness.

The narrator-witness writes the Prologue, Chapters I, II, IV, VII, and the Epilogue. He outlines the theories of Amaranto and Escobar as well as those of Lario and Lirio, the disputing scene viewers of Chapter II. In a sense, he is another character, existing on the same plane as the others: for him Amaranto, Escobar, Lario, Lirio, Don Guillén, and "la Pinta" are real people and their story has historical substance. He writes in the first person and pretends to be putting down his own recollections of actual persons and events, supplementing this first-hand knowledge with information supplied by others: "la Pinta" and Guillén tell about Belarmino and Apolonio; in Escobar's papers he finds a partial vocabulary of Belarmino's language. He maintains the pretense of real life by confessing his inability to understand some of the people he meets, especially Don Guillén ("a él no le comprendía. ¿Qué era aquel hombre que ante mí estaba...?" p. 25). Because he moves in the same "real" world he is describing, this narrator can take part in the drama's action. No mere spectator, he intervenes in the lives of Guillén and "la Pinta" when, in Chapter VII, he brings them together again and thereby becomes the *deus ex machina* of his own tale. But the trials and tribulations of the lovers are, according to the narrator's avowal, only the background for the more important history of their fathers, the prodigious shoemakers, Belarmino and Apolonio (p. 26); yet he himself, while referring to it as if it were a matter of common knowledge, does not present that central action.

It is the omniscient narrator who, in Chapters III, V, VIII, tells the main story. He differs from the narrator-witness not only in the depth and range of his vision but also in his attitude towards the material; unlike his alter ego, he does not intrude, either by appearing as an actor within the fiction, or by interrupting its course with personal opinions (nor does he ever refer to himself as "I"). The point of view in these chapters is not that of a self-conscious writer who addresses himself to his readers, but that of an "invisible" and feignedly impartial one whose presence can be felt only in the irony of his tone. Curiously, he seems scarcely aware of what happens in the chapters told by his fellow narrator — and entirely ignorant of the reminiscences of Don Guillén. His omniscience does not extend to the feelings and thoughts of Pedro and Angustias, for although the turning point in the main story is their elopement, he records only the reactions of Belarmino and Apolonio.

Don Guillén's long monologue, directed to the narrator-witness and taking up almost all of Chapters IV and VII, furnishes the subjective version of that elopement. A character who tells about his own drama might be called a narrator-actor. Paradoxically, although he speaks in the first person, his account is more indirect than that of the omniscient author; whereas the latter can show thoughts and feelings dramatically, as they occur, the former must recollect them from a more or less remote past; between the narrator-actor and his tale stands a barrier of time and self-interest. Don Guillén is the only character permitted to disclose his inner life in his own words, yet, because of certain incongruities and the conflicting opinions of others, that inner self is never clearly visible to the reader. Since the author gives us no inside view, the priest's personality seems blurred and ambiguous.

The three narrators refer to happenings on two different time levels: the action in Madrid (told by the narrator-witness) takes place in six days, from Tuesday of Holy Week to Easter Sunday; the action in Pilares (told by the omniscient author) stretches over a period of eight years but ends several years before the Madrid episodes. Don Guillén's monologue, chronicling everything from his childhood in Pilares to his encounter with the narrator-witness in Madrid, covers both time series. The two levels then converge in the last two chapters when, on Easter Sunday, Angustias and

Pedro are reunited (Chapter VII) and Belarmino and Apolonio reconciled (Chapter VIII).

The omniscient author uses the standard fictive present (with verbs in the past tense): locating the "now" in the very progression of the plot, he does not hint at future consequences but allows the characters to enact the drama before the reader's eyes. On the other hand, both Don Guillén and the narrator-witness, separated in time from what they tell, summarize events from the vantage point of the present: the latter emphasizes the temporal gap when he says that he want to salvage this particular story (one of many almost lost in memory's "río de sombras") from the limbo of his own forgetfulness ("Hoy me siento en humor de salvar del olvido un drama...", 16). Because a narrator who sees everything as ended long ago cannot maintain the illusion of an unpredictable present unfolding before the reader, the melodrama of Angustias and Pedro is essentially undramatic. The author does, however, impart a certain suspense to its reconstruction by interrupting it with the chapters dealing with Belarmino and Apolonio, thus at once delaying the disclosure of the lovers' tragedy and anticipating its key episodes.

The shifts from one narrator to another and from one temporal plane to a more remote one, segment the plot so that some incidents are told twice while others are given only indirect mention. One speaker may allude to happenings not yet recorded, another may refer in passing to a situation that is elsewhere thoroughly developed in the narrative or acted out in dramatic scene. For example, the history of the growth and spread of Belarminian thought among Pilares' intellectuals is thus fragmented and anticipated: between Angustias' reference to her father's following among the university students in Chapter I and the occurrences with which the omniscient narrator begins Chapter III (Bellido's threats, the arrival of an as yet unknown rival, and the beginning of the most metaphysical phase of Belarmino's thought), there is a backward time-shift of several years; Guillén first speaks of Belarmino in connection with his linguistic theories (Chapter IV, p. 68), but he notes the shoemaker's numerous university disciples; not until Chapter V (p. 94) does the omniscient author thoroughly detail in the narrative Belarmino's rise to popularity among the students. Various other episodes in his life are likewise splintered into the disconnected reports of persons who recall them from different time levels. The omniscient author prepares for the tie between the shoemaker and the Neira family in Chapter III (p. 57); in Chapter IV Guillén briefly mentions it when telling about his friendship with Angustias (p. 75); in Chapter V the omniscient author takes up Belarmino's life after the financial ruin that forced him to set up his shop in a doorway of the Neira mansion (pp. 81, 83-84). The collapse of Belarmino's business never appears in the narrative, for it occurs between Chapters III and V (Chapter IV being Don Guillén's monologue). So too, the philosopher-shoemaker's discovery of "la solera recreada" and his subsequent psychological transformation are not directly shown either in dramatic scene or narrative summary; they can only be inferred from retrospective remarks.

By giving two versions of an incident, the author can show it both from within and from without, subjectively and objectively, or he can portray the distinctive effects of a certain event on different characters. The tone of the narrative may change from tragic to comic as the author treats his personages first sympathetically, then ironically. The turning point in the lives of both pairs of characters, Belarmino-Apolonio, Pedro-Angustias, is the elopement of the latter. In Chapter VI the omniscient author tells about it in order to show the reactions of the shoemakers, reactions that parody the solutions offered by "el drama y la filosofía" (the title of the chapter). Since in the drama of Belarmino and Apolonio the sentiments of Angustias and Pedro are relatively unimportant, the author focuses only on the thoughts and acts of the shoemakers. But in Chapter VII ("Pedrito y Angustias"), Don Guillén recounts the episode as protagonist: now the mad cobblers recede into the background while the feelings of the actor-narrator occupy the foreground. The subjective and objective elements in the two stories are reversible: we enter the comedy of Belarmino and Apolonio after passing through the melodrama that frames it; the heroes of the frame-story, Guillén and "la Pinta" then reappear —with different names, Pedrito and Angustias— in the central action. The novel turns inside out, from tragedy or melodrama to comedy and then back again.

In the subordinate actions too, the author presents both internal and external views; he does this not by changing narrators but by abrupt shifts from dramatic scene, in which a character speaks out directly, to an impersonal narrative summary of his behavior. Each of the minor characters is made at some moment the protagonist of a miniature drama — and then relegated to the supporting cast. The actors are constantly exchanging positions on the novel's stage: the hero in one scene becomes a silent onlooker in another. As if to demonstrate Don Amaranto's assertion that "cada vida es un drama de más o menos intensidad" (14), or Apolonio's belief in the tragic conflict hidden within each inhabitant of the Rúa Ruera (103), Pérez de Ayala lets each one take a turn in uncovering his inward self.[2] But what is lived by the character as a personal tragedy is seen from without as grotesque farce. This duality is extended by using the subordinate action as a counterpoint to the primary one: the frustrated love affair of Felicita Quemada and Anselmo Novillo serves as a tragicomic foil to the love story of Pedro and Angustias. The author duplicates and reverses the patterns of his plot, altering both the perspective and the emotional tone.

The Multifaceted Picture of Character

The description of personality in this novel is never unitary. Everyone appears in terms of at least two inconsonant traits which may be succintly given in a two-part sentence: "Celedonio de Obeso, ateo declarado y republicano agresivo; en el fondo un pedazo de pan, un zoquete" (p. 19). Even the characters comment on the surprising contrasts between inner and outer reality: the Duchess of Somavia says of Novillo, "Parece mentira que este hombre temible en las elecciones que a todos sacaba ventaja en maquinar un chanchullo y sacarlo adelante por redaños, fuese, en el fondo, la criatura más simple, candorosa, sentimental y asustadiza" (p. 139). Guillén describes Felicita as "alma jugosa y

---

[2] In the Introduction of the 1942 edition of *Troteras y danzaderas* (Buenos Aires), the author distinguished two functions for secondary or episodic characters: one, to provoke or stimulate the protagonist to action, the other, "representar la diversidad de las actitudes fundamentales frente a la vida, enfrentadas por tanto entre sí, con que el personaje episódico pasa a ser, cada cual a su turno y en su presente, personaje principal" (p. 6).

generosa como la vid buena revestida de un tronco sarmentoso y casi momia" (p. 158). Inner contradictions may be symbolized by a sexual ambivalence, formulated in a symmetrical verbal pattern: Anselmo Novillo is called "el Buey", "quizás por su corpulencia, tal vez por satírica suspicacia" (p. 49); padre Alesón's voice sounds "más de monja que de fraile" (p. 84); Felicita "vista por la espalda, era una figurilla breve, fina y graciosa. El anverso de la medalla no se correspondía con el dorso; pecho alisado con rasero... una faz del todo masculina" (p. 47). Another concise formulation of the incompatible qualities fused in one person is an oxymoron in which the order of the two terms is reversible: Guillén says about Belarmino, "no sé si era un loco cuerdo o un cuerdo loco" (p. 68).

By presenting a person through the sharply divergent judgements of his fellows, the author paradigmatically exemplifies the innumerable views that compose one's social self.[3] Each evaluates the other on the basis of entirely different standards. And this multiplicity is abbreviated in the form of an antithesis: the narrator-witness is attracted by Angustias's sweetness and innocence (she looks like "una virgen de Rafael, algo ajada", 20), but one of the other prostitutes criticizes this innocence as professional ineptitude; the conflict of opinions condenses into a stylistic clash: "Era una mujer dulce, triste, y reconcentrada, o según el tecnicismo de la Piernavieja, una simple que no servía *pal* caso" (p. 21). The narrator-witness wonders about Don Guillén and mentally reviews all the possible interpretations of his character: "¿Qué era aquel hombre que ante mí estaba, deglutiendo y racionando al propio tiempo, masticando y discurriendo, con tanta frialdad, escrúpulo y elegancia... ¿Un hedionista? ¿Un incrédulo? ¿Un hipócrita y un sofista, para consigo mismo y los demás? ¿Un desengañado? ¿Un atormentado?" (p. 25; the observer's simultaneous awareness

---

[3] Pérez de Ayala is more interested in calling attention to the splintering of opinion about a character than in developing the complexities of consciousness. In this he differs from other relativists like Gide or, more recently, Lawrence Durrell. In *The Alexandria Quartet*, Durrell provides for each main character a succession of radically distinct interpretations, analyses, and revelations that progressively disclose all the contradictory features of personality. Pérez de Ayala prefers a laconic summary of divergent views; he represents the many-sidedness of reality through linguistic symmetries rather than through a wealth of psychological observation.

of physical and mental activities is another example of the double view). Guillén's elusiveness is signified by a plurality of names. Since each name suggests a different kind of person, the priest lets his acquaintances choose whichever one best suits their preconceptions:

> —"Me llamo Pedro, Lope, Francisco, Guillén, Eurípides; a elegir.

* * *

> —Unos me llaman por uno, otros por otro. Use usted el que prefiere.
> —Pues, prefiero don Guillén.
> —Es el que suelen preferir las señoras —dijo don Guillén con dejo satírico.
> —Por mi parte, si usted me lo permite, le designaré como señor Eurípides; me sabe a república —entró a decir don Celedonio de Obeso, ateo declarado y republicano agresivo." (Pp. 18-19.)

In describing his father, Guillén allows the same freedom of choice to his listeners; "mi padre... era autor dramático y zapatero, o zapatero y autor dramático, según el orden de prelación que usted prefiera" (18). From this first reference, the reader's picture of Apolonio is built up piecemeal from comments of others. Angustias is most impressed with the shoemaking fame of her lover's father: "Apolonio Caramanzana. Le habrá oído usted mentar. ¡Ah! era el mejor zapatero de España... Además componía dramas" (p. 22). In Chapter III the omniscient author, ignoring these anticipatory allusions, prepares his own introduction of the cobbler through a summary of the gossip on the Rúa Ruera. The gradual fitting together of pertinent facts realized by the inhabitants of the street is a model of the reader's own bit by bit accumulation of descriptive elements. When Apolonio finally makes his entrance, he is pictured through Belarmino's eyes as "un hombre lo más híspido y enchipado, bigotes tiesos, sombrero sobre una oreja, flor en el ojal, chaquet de largos faldones y que, en conjunto, a Belarmino le produjo una impresión soñada, desagradable y epicena, entre chulo y pavo real" (p. 58). Later this same image is recalled by Don Guillén who modifies its affective coloring: "había que verle lo pomposo y majetón, con su flor en el ojal, su sombrero ladeado y su chaquet, un chaquet paradisíaco, como decía el conde" (p. 64).

The character who elicits the most varied reactions is Belarmino. He too grows by accretion, emerging from the pronouncements and sentiments of others. Angustias defends his saintliness against her mother's unjust denigrations (p. 21). The omniscient author refers to the disparities in community opinion:

> El sastre Balmisa, el director y redactores de *La Aurora*... tomaban a broma a Belarmino y le calificaban de chiflado. El clero y las familias piadosas le reputaban como un loco... Pero el estado llano del partido, obreros y artesanos humildes, dedicaban a Belarmino supersticiosa fe y se enardecían oyéndole (p. 52).

Don Guillén confesses he has never been able to understand him ("Yo no sé si era un loco cuerdo o un cuerdo loco", p. 68); Padre Alesón asserts that he lacks a rational soul, and the omniscient author, in a rare intrusion, contradicts the priest ("Como Belarmino, aunque el padre Alesón le reputase insensato, era un hombre muy sensato", p. 89). Eventually all Pilares is torn by the heated polemic between *belarmistas y anti-belarmistas*.

Reality and Fiction

The split in the author's narrative personality not only provides divergent perspectives on the story but creates within it two levels of reality: the pseudo-real world of the narrator-witness (Madrid) incloses the more obviously imaginary one (Pilares) of the omniscient author (Madrid keeps its real name, but Oviedo is disguised as Pilares). In the Prologue and the first two chapters, the first person speaker talks about the characters as if they were real people, and in the epilogue, he maintains this pretense by referring to the information derived from Escobar's notes which have fallen into his hands (the device of the "found manuscript" thus accounts for a small portion of the novel). He accentuates the independence of the people he describes by setting up and never resolving the conflict between Amaranto and Escobar's interpretations (he denies, as, we have noted, holding any specific theory of his own about the two shoemakers). Yet when "la Pinta" and Don Guillén appear in the omniscient narrator's story, the pretended historicity of the first two chapters is undermined. Persons the author has met turn into characters in a novel, and novelistic characters are spoken of as if they were real acquaintances. The action is reported first as fact, then as fiction; life and literature seem to merge.

By destroying the boundaries between the real world and the invented one, the author shows the whole novel to be a made up thing. Instead of drawing the reader into the story so that he momentarily forgets that it is just a wordy fabrication, Pérez de Ayala deliberately makes him aware of its literary nature. Already in the Prologue, he indicates that he is far more than a mere reporter: "Pero hoy me siento en humor de salvar del olvido un drama semipatético, semiburlesco, de cuyos interesantes elementos una parte me la ofreció el acaso, otra la fui acopiando en años de investigación y perseverante rebusca. Por eso lo considero caso como una obra original mía", (p. 16). In emphasizing the novel's capricious origin, he calls attention to his own creative role.[4] Nevertheless, when he begins to tell the story, this narrator-witness pretends to be an observer of actual events, limited in his knowledge of the characters and their motives; he would have us believe that his is just one of many possible versions. The ruse, of course, cannot be examined too closely, and in the epilogue it is abandoned completely when the narrator announces to the reader that he himself is the novel's maker. "Belarmino y Apolonio han existido, y yo los he amado. No digo que hayan existido en carne mortal sobre el haz de la tierra; han existido por mí y para mí" (p. 193).[5] He shows his characters for what they are, not creatures of flesh and blood but figures invented to stand for certain ideal positions.

---

[4] Leo Spitzer, in "Perspectivismo lingüístico en El Quijote", in *Lingüística e historia literaria* (Madrid, 1955), p. 217, cites the *Quijote's* famous first words as a declaration of the artist's freedom and traces this form of "narración subjetiva" in related opening passages of Goethe, Sterne, Fielding, Melville, E. M. Forster.

[5] The words echo those of the "prudentísimo Cide Hamete Benegeli": "Para mí solo nació Don Quijote, y yo para él: él supo obrar, y yo escribir: solos los dos somos para en uno." Charles Leighton, in "The Structure of *Belarmino y Apolonio*," *Bulletin of Hispanic Studies*, XXXVII (1960), 241, observes that Pérez de Ayala's perspectivism, like Cervantes's, is unified by the personality of the artist.

Holding together the novel's multiple points of view is the unifying perspective of the author.

Pérez de Ayala has here devised a complicated mechanism of interchanging parts: two theorists argue about two opposing ways of understanding human reality; three narrators report the action which is divided into two separate but related plots; events take place on two different time levels and are described from distinct points of view, sometimes as fact, sometimes as fiction. The structural complexity perfectly embodies the theme of plural realities. The theory of the double view, introduced in the Prologue and developed in regards to fiction in Chapter II, turns out to be the compositional principle of the entire work.

Relativism and Humor

The author has given form to his perspectivistic vision in the intricacies of style and structure; the novel is a carefully wrought image of the relativity of truth. Yet at the center of his ingenious contrivance is an absurd story about two crazy shoemakers, and in this incongruity Pérez de Ayala indicates his final devasting judgement of ideological endeavors. In the Prologue, Amaranto observes that the rise of rationalism destroyed man's previously unified approach to the world; reason confined itself to a physical realm deprived of transcendence and meaning, while religion took over a spiritual realm devoid of substance. The sciences do not allow a grasp of total reality because they fragment the study of matter into unrelated collections of facts. Therefore, says Don Amaranto, the only avenues to knowledge in the modern world are drama and philosophy. Escobar shares this belief, and the author, in so far as he adopts the notions of both in composing his novel, also seems to support this view. But then since Belarmino and Apolonio are the persons who exemplify these "disciplines," the cognitive values of drama and philosophy become rather doubtful. If the shoemaker's pursuits are our last hope, any effort to make the world intelligible would seem to be vain and ridiculous (*Bouvard et Pécuchet* had shown "the failings of the sciences;" the Spanish novel shows the failings of the humanities). But this comic devaluation points to yet another way of integrating experience and reducing the chaos of infinite realities to human measure —at the same time protecting the fragile superstructure of ideas from the corrosive effects of simplemindedness— humor.

The comic mode provides a particularly appropriate expression of a thoroughgoing relativism. Relativistic thought is not essentially or invariably humorous, but humor is invariably relativizing and critical. Comedy arises from an abrupt shift in the angle of vision that converts the meaningful into the utterly meaningless; it is the affective or emotional destruction of false values, and to the mocking and distrustful humorist, *all* values are pompous errors. Precisely because he makes fun of inflexible positions and narrow ideologies, the humorist can accept and affirm all the conflicting parts of reality. Pérez de Ayala rejects any single view, demonstrating by the confrontation of opposites, the insufficiency of all mental constructions. If there are as many irreducible truths as there are points of view, every pretension to absolute truth is comical.

The novel's humor springs from the critical treatment of a number of ideas and theories. By counterbalancing the theses of Amaranto and Escobar, the author shows their truth to be relative; by illustrating those theses with the story of Belarmino and Apolonio, he shows them to be slightly ludicrous as well. So too, he gives an ironic tone to the discussion of the novelist's craft by putting it into the mouth of Don Amaranto. The linguistic theme, so ingeniously developed through Belarmino's philosophy, also appears in comic guise: the principles and assumptions that underlie the shoemaker's linguistic system are perfectly serious (several studies have compared Belarmino's speculations to those of Mallarmé, Max Müller, Charles Bally, and Martin Heidegger),[6] but Pérez de Ayala humorously qualifies them, making his very real concern with language the subject of farce. *Belarmino y Apolonio* is a novel of ideas, and ideas, Don Amaranto says, are only biological emanations, "vapores de la carne efímera" (p. 11), arbitrary and capricious notions best treated with the playful superiority of comedy. Indeed, the novelistic genre, which Ortega y Gasset

---

[6] Belarmino's language is discussed in the next chapter.

describes as essentially comic and critical,[7] might be the most appropriate setting for an analysis of these intellectual conceits. If, as Ortega claims, the realistic novel depicts the fall of the myth, the disintegration of the ideal at the touch of inert, senseless reality, then this work is a model of its class: methodically the author devaluates every thought, every conjectural system put forth in the book, until the very esteem we hold for reason seems an absurd delusion. But if rationality is made fun of, so is religion. The temporal frame of the novel is an impious inversion of Christian symbol: the events leading up to the happy ending of the love story take place during Holy Week; the prostitute Angustias is restored to her lover, a priest, on Easter Sunday; her redemption is accomplished through human, not divine love. The narrator describes their reunion in religious terms: the scene reproduces "la imagen emotiva que con línea ingénua y tintas traslúcidas bosquejaron los santos melodas del Breviario" (p. 171). Reason and faith turn out to be equally inadequate approaches to life.

When both knowledge and religion are impossible, what remains? In the Epilogue the first-person narrator affirms life's non-rational values: "Eso es todo. Existir, multiplicarse y amar" (p. 193). This formula had been previously voiced by Belarmino: "El tetraedo [el todo] es un sueño. Sólo es verdad el amor, el bien, la amistad" (p. 187). By making the crazy shoemaker the spokesman for his own beliefs, Pérez de Ayala fuses comedy and a doctrine of love. Love and comedy, the often paired gestures of affirmation, bring together the infinite fragments of reality.

---

[7] "El género novelesco es, sin duda, cómico... Se trata simplemente de aprovechar la significación poética que hay en la caída violenta del cuerpo trágico, vencido por la fuerza de la inercia, por la realidad"; "El arte novelesco es un género de intención crítica y cómico nervio", José Ortega y Gasset, *Meditaciones del Quijote*, 3rd. ed. (Madrid, 1922), pp. 188 and 191.

Chapter III

LINGUISTIC PERSPECTIVISM

Because of its inherent ambiguity, language occupies a central place among Pérez de Ayala's relativistic themes. He is concerned both with the individual expressive act and with the effect that words may have on the "real" material world; both of these topics are part of a more general one, the relation between the artist and his creation or the interpenetration of literature and life. The novelist shows through language the relativity, instability, and reversibility of subjective experience and objective fact. Fascinated with the diversity of meanings a word may have, he engages in all kinds of verbal conceits and frequently extends this word-play from the texture of the prose to the structure of a scene or an entire plot. When the author's own speech is ironic, meaning emerges indirectly, so that a phrase or sentence acquires a double dimension and facilitates what Belarmino calls "una visión bilateral, de doble fondo". The characters in these works are themselves intrigued by the charms and complexities of language: they talk about the multivalency of words, judge the vocabulary and style of their fellows, evince a passion for naming —or nicknaming— and even go so far as to create new, private idioms.

The Language of the Characters

Pérez de Ayala often focuses on the achievement or failure of the expressive act. Common in these fictions is the complete frustration of communication; many characters barely manage to speak, while others adopt a phraseology so unusual and inept as to completely disconcert their listeners. Tigre Juan is immured by passions he is unable to give vent to in speech ("Su caracter tímido y taciturno le impedía expansionarse, desahogar. Iba agriándose en su corazón. El suplicio mudo se le hacía insufrible", *Tigre Juan*, p. 160); he envies Vespasiano's agile rhetoric ("se acordó de la melodiosa fluidez, de ruiseñor en celo, de Vespasiano, su otro yo", *Curandero*, p. 27). The unhappy scholar-tutor, Don Cástulo, never seems able to make an audible transcript of his splendid internal monologues which "eran siempre en este estilo frondoso y altisonante, así como su lenguaje articulado era muchas veces desmedrado y premioso" (*Trabajos*, p. 95). When a person does succeed in articulating, his words mysteriously invert his intention. Precisely because of the plurality of significance, language not only distorts emotion but also serves as the perfect medium of deception: Vespasiano illustrates the bewitching effects of verbal duplicity. If speech misleads, then silence must be the vehicle of truth; Don Sincerato's deaf-mutes "sing," "La verdad es como el aire / transparente y cristalina... La mentira / tiene voz. En el silencio largo, la verdad anida" (*Curandero*, p. 26).

Pérez de Ayala sees the effect of language as two-fold; not only does it translate and transform the inner world but, in a sense, it establishes and creates the external one. Since words are the conveyors of concepts, and since concepts provide the categories and conditions of experience, language interpenetrates with reality. Pérez de Ayala's characters, like children and primitives, identify word and object so closely that speech becomes magical incantation. To the spell-bound listener, words solidify into palpable objects: "Escuchaba como los niños acostumbran, con los ojos, como si las palabras, al desgajarse de los labios, se materializasen, adquiriendo la forma y color de los objetos representados. Veía los vocablos en su religiosa desnudez originaria" (*Troteras*, p. 72). The abstractions designated in speech are also substantialized: "Doña Micaela y doña Iluminada, que escuchaban con los labios en hechura de O, murmuraron al tiempo, como si las palabras del cura se les hubieran introducido desprevenidamente en la boca, y luego de paladear la pulpa sustantífica, se apresuraron a expulsar la almendra" (*Curandero*, p. 10). The materialized word may shatter into concrete phonetic fragments as when "el puñado de letras que éste tenía en la boca se le convirtió en una masa indeglutible de cacofonías" (*Prometeo*, p. 58). Even the written word personifies itself: "Cada palabra de aquella carta había retumbado dentro de su cráneo como un trompetazo del Juicio Final... Más que palabras eran seres vivos, o resucitados, que se desplegaban como un regimiento disciplinado, ante Tigre Juan (*Tigre*, p. 155). The narrator revives and extends dead metaphors so that a "dead language" may suffer physical dissolution: Padre Alesón knew "veinte idiomas: unos vivos, otros muertos y otros putrefactos" (*Belarmino*, p. 55).

Because words can mold events and determine action, the characters hold names in superstitious awe. A man's name can decide his fate: the hero of *Prometeo*, changes his name from the plebeyan Juan Pérez to Marco de Setiñano ("Juan Pérez le parecía un conjuro vehemente a la Némesis plebeya," p. 38); when "Grano de Pimienta" is nicknamed "el Diputadín," his life is so altered that he runs away from the valley of Congosto (*Ombligo*); the seven dreadful sisters in *Los trabajos de Urbano y Simona* vainly try to evade the evil influence of their names (Práxedes, Leónidas, Onofre, Arsenia, Sulforiana, Trifona, Degollación), their "mal sino" (p. 175). The proliferation of nicknames in all the fictions is a short-hand representation of collective and individual judgements. The characters, all enthusiastic nominalists, refuse to accept the designations of an unthinking tradition that has reduced the rich variety of human types to the limited groupings of impersonal proper names. They invent new aliases to express their consensus of opinion. The nickname, usually based on appearance or on some external accident, is a mask painted by one's acquaintances; "Los apodos son, cuándo biografía sucinta, cuándo retrato en miniatura" (*Belarmino*, p. 91). Some people have more than one *apodo*, reflecting different aspects of their personality or physiognomy: Froilán Escobar is both "el estudiantón" (a biographical name) and "Aligator" (a portrait name). Juan Guerra de Madrigal ("pareja nada compatible de apellidos" in which unreal, purely linguistic entities clash) is called "Tigre Juan, por su traza hosca y su carácter insociable" (p. 19) and "Curandero de su honra" because of the legend about his past and his appearances in the title role of Calderón's drama. When the community perceives a new resemblance, it may change the alias and consequently its opinion of the person, for evalutions are grounded in a system of imagined similarities: " 'Grano de Pimienta' y 'Mil Perdones' " traces the reversal in the fortunes of two young men subsequent to their receiving new *apodos*.

The novelist satirizes all intellectual endeavor as empty verbalism (Apolonio's poetic dramas are hollow artifices of misused words; Belarmino's philosophy is an insanely logical linguistic system). The onomastic obsession of his characters is the model of all wordy activities—philosophy, theology, etc.:

> Como los habitantes del valle apenas han tenido nada que hacer desde las edades protohistóricas, se han ido entreteniendo en inventar nombres para todo lo que veían... De esta comezón nominalista han adolecido siempre los que llevan vida recoleta y ociosa; que no es otro el origen de muchas teologías, filosofías y sociologías, agudas y vanas (*Ombligo*, pp. 11-12).

Man is imprisoned within the confines of sensory perception, but he imagines that external reality corresponds to the symbolic network of language. Although names and terms are completely arbitrary, he confidently uses them to make a chimerical replica of the world. "Los hombres, / detrás de su prisión. ¿Qué sabes? / cuando más, a las cosas has puesto sendos nombres" (*Ombligo*, p. 7).

Because each way of speaking indicates a unique approach to reality, the novelist can signify diverse points of view by multiplying private idioms. Even the character whose personality is only rudimentarily developed has his own peculiar mode of expression. The linguistic perspective is original even when the human being behind it remains in shadow. Just as a dehumanized mask replaces a real person, so too a disembodied voice may point to the existence of an attitude not otherwise delineated. The proliferation of speech styles suggests more the verbal playfulness of the author than the psychological diversity of the characters.[1] Specialized,

---

[1] But this great expressive variety can only lead to misunderstanding between men; the babel of tongues is part of a general incomprehension and confusion:

> Cada hombre que es una cosa de veras, habla un idioma distinto, que no entiende el que no es esa cosa, porque tienen alma distinta...

more or less hermetic languages abound. Many characters cultivate an elevated style, for example, the well-read servant in *Pata de la raposa* (who is particularly attracted to works on philosophy, ethics, and sociology "porque los entendía menos") has accumulated a pompous vocabulary that he himself does not understand ("La contumelia de las circunstancias es la base más firme de la metempsicosis," (p. 34); Padre Paloma (*Trabajos*) laces his conversation with sentences and paragraphs in Latin; Don Cástulo's language is obscure and erudite. In "La triste Ariadne," the illiterate "Xuanín el Sapo" composes abstruse poetry much admired by some of the town's intellectuals. These characters constantly bewilder their hearers: Don Telesforo Hurtado cannot understand "el lenguaje rebuscadamente culto de Alberto" (*Pata*, p. 42); Doña Micaela and Rosita are unable to follow Don Cástulo's ornate phraseology and mythological references, nor his quotations in Latin and Greek (which Rosita takes for Basque); Conchona's family comprehend not a single word of his magnificently phrased request for their daughter's hand in marriage (Conchona's dialect translation furnishes that stylistic contrast so common in these novels: "quier decise, hablando en cristiano, que el señorín cásase conmigo" (*Trabajos*, p. 96).

All the personages in *Tigre Juan, El Curandero de su honra*, and *Belarmino* are linguistically characterized. Don Sincerato Gamborena, director of a school for deaf mutes, speaks in short, elliptical phrases combined for alliteration and consonant rhyme; his sayings are like those children's nonsense rhymes that spring from a delight in word connections suggested by sound alone. [2] Nachín de Nacha makes his Asturian dialect a poetic medium. Tigre Juan, trained in the theater, handles two styles, a high style and the local vernacular; indeed, he is so linguistically sophisticated (when

---

El mundo es como una gran lonja, llena de sordos que aspiran a verificar sus transacciones; todos gritan; hay un horrendo rebullicio; pero como no se oyen los unos a los otros, no se concluye ningún trato. (*Belarmino*, p. 112.)

[2] "— ¡Cuajo, guanajo, cáscaras de ajo!— chilló el clérigo, que manejaba surtido repertorio de exclamaciones por aliteración y consonancia. Coria, Babia, Batuecas; allí se está Tigre Juan. Con as en manc no arrastra. Las cuarenta doña Marica. Dos perronas perdidas en tonto. ¡Ejem! ¡Ejem! ¡Ejem! Tigre Juan, mientes ausentes. ¡Ja! ¡Ja! ¡Ja! Alerta, tuerta, detrás de la puerta. Gamborena, presente. Oros veinte. Perra gorda. *Sursum corda*. (*Tigre*, p. 177.)

not trying to describe his own feelings) that he can adjust his speech to the intelligence and social position of his interlocutor, shifting from elegant diction to dialect (*Tigre*, p. 26). Though theatrical and pompous himself, he admonishes others for lack of simplicity and clarity (pp. 211-12); he has a predilection for contrived forms, a taste shared by Doña Iluminada who is fond of aphorisms and rhetorical similies ("Como gonce y cerrojo en un postigo, que no abre sin el uno, ni sin el otro cierra, así el querer de la mujer y el hombre. Amor y matrimonio: si falta el cerrojo, que es la voluntad del varón, es puerta abierta e inútil; puerta falsa sin el gonce, que es la voluntad de la mujer," *Tigre*, p. 80).

In *Belarmino y Apolonio*, Colignon's argot is a mixture of French and Spanish; Aloponio finds it all but impossible to speak in prose instead of verse; Felicita's locutions betray the influence of the *folletines* she reads; Don Guillén sometimes lapses into the preacher's oratory (the narrator recognizes it as such and excuses it: "Yo, naturalmente, juzgué espontánea, sincera y, por lo tanto, lícita en la ocasión, la pequeña expansión retórica de don Guillén," p. 169); Padre Alesón tries to win Belarmino's confidence with convoluted and ingenious phraseology ("hablaba ahora en este estilo conceptuoso y envuelto, para dar por el gusto a Belarmino y granjearse su afecto," p. 92). But Belarmino's is the most striking verbal originality, for he not only makes up a new language but devises a complicated theoretical apparatus to explain and regulate its growth.

Belarmino's Language

The shoemaker's linguistic is not a mere subsidiary of his philosophy. Rather, his philosophy *is* language theory.[3] In this

---

[3] Belarmino's language has been the subject of several studies. Bernard Levy, in "Pérez de Ayala's *Belarmino y Apolonio*", *Spanish Review*, III (1936), 80, refers to the author's "scornful disdain of Belarmino's hermetic idiom," which he compares to Mallarmé's in that both "enlarge language with greater burdens than it can bear." Carlos Clavería, in "Apostillas al lenguaje de Belarmino", *Cinco estudios de la literatura española moderna* (Salamanca, 1945), p. 77, relates the novelist's interest in language to the theories of Max Müller, concluding that "Belarmino parece aspirar, en el fondo, a la esencialidad, a una identificación de las palabras y las cosas, del pensamiento que les da realidad y del lenguaje que las expresa". Charles

thoroughly idealistic system language not only molds experience but actually brings into existence the world of things. For Belarmino, the act of knowledge is a fresh and unique perception that requires giving the object a new name, and the name, in turn, founds or creates reality: "la cosa y la palabra es uno mismo; nacen las cosas cuando nacen las palabras; sin palabras no hay cosas... porque la cosa no existe por sí ni para otras cosas..., sino que existe solamente para un *Inteleto* que la conoce, y en cuanto que la conoce le da un nombre, le pone una palabra. Conocer es crear, y crear es conocer" (p. 86). Knowledge is creation, and creation is linguistic originality. But as ordinarily used, words are mere conventions that allow no insight into the nature of thing: "En el cosmos — es decir, en el diccionario — están los nombres de todas las cosas, pero están mal aplicados, porque están aplicados según costumbre mecánica y en forma que, lejos de

---

Leighton, in "La parodia en *Belarmino y Apolonio*", *Hispanófila*, 6 (1959), 55, says that Belarmino is a parody of philosophers in general and of the Krausists in particular, and that furthermore this parody is magnified to include "todos los que al buscar una terminología precisa, sea lo que fuere su propósito, inventan una lengua hermética" — certain lawyers, sociologists, psychologists, and poets. María del Carmen Bobes, in "Notas a *Belarmino y Apolonio* de Pérez de Ayala", *Boletín del Instituto de Estudios Asturianos*, XXXIV (1958), writes about the novel's linguistic perspectivism ("lo inesperado de las asociaciones que llevan a Belarmino a sustituir un término por otro tiene un efecto inmediato, la comicidad, pero tiene otro más especial: demostrar un desdoblamiento, una posibilidad de situarse en ángulos distintos para apreciar cualquier argumento humano"); she compares the author's approach to Charles Bally's conception of language as a system of "clichés hechos" and shows how Belarmino's methods are "los mismos en que se basa la lengua corriente en sus evoluciones de tipo semántico" (318). Carla Cordua de Torreti, in "Belarmino: hablar y pensar", *La Torre*, 32 (1960), 43-60, finds a resemblance between the shoemaker's opposition to common speech and Heidegger's account of the degeneration of "el habla" into "habladuría"; she describes the metaphorical and creative origin of all language that is reproduced in Belarmino's private tongue. It is not really so absurd as it may seem to consider the speculations of the crazy but ingenious cobbler against the background of modern linguistic theories because, as María del Carmen Bobes points out, "Todos los puntos que la moderna lingüística estudia aparecen en referencia a la validez de la lengua del zapatero filósofo, y todos ellos pasan a convertirse en material artístico en manos de Pérez de Ayala, vistos desde el ángulo de la intuición, no del discurso" (216). The principles and assumptions at the root of Belarmino's verbal inventiveness are perfectly serious, though their development is comic; we remember that in this book all ideas, including the author's own, are undermined by humor.

provocar un acto de conocimiento y de creación, favorecen la rutina, la ignorancia, la estupidez, la charlatanería..." (p. 87). Belarmino would remake words, stretching and expanding their significance to include all the meanings suggested by sound or association of ideas: "El aquel de la filosofía no es más que enanchar las palabras" (p. 42). Thus expanded, words can reveal all kinds of otherwise hidden relationships, tying together the most diverse objects and concepts. The dictionary is to Belarmino an epitome of the universe, "clave con que descifrar los más insospechados enigmas" (p. 86). Each word with its cluster of meanings or connotations provides a multiple view of reality: polysemy is the linguistic expression of perspectivism.

The origin of the shoemaker's language repeats the probable origin of all human speech: a particular vocal sound begins by being primarily connotative, suggesting feelings and vague ideas. With Belarmino this process is deliberate and he carefully avoids the next step, the condensation of meaning to denote a single object ("A Belarmino le gustó la voz expeditivo y la almacenó en la memoria, a fin de meterla en la horma, ensancharla y darle un significado espacioso, nuevo y conveniente," (p. 57). He wants to prevent the simple pairing of a word and its referent ("me aplaco haciendo hormas para varios pies y enanchando palabras para varias cosas, cuanto más, mejor," p. 42). His vocabulary is therefore inexact, elastic, and ambiguous. Indeed, ambiguity is so much the essence of his thought that the sense of certain words lurks behind a dense cloud of connotations that Belarmino himself cannot penetrate. For example, "bilateral," which appears in the name of his shop ("El Nenrod boscoso y equitativo. Zapatería bilateral de Belarmino Pinto"), is extremely evocative but does not lend itself to precise elucidation: "Como filósofo catecúmeno, Belarmino empleaba algunos términos a los cuales daba valor místico, y cuyo contenido no hubiera acertado jamás a elucidar" (p. 43). [4]

The shoemaker's private lexicon consists of two kinds of multi-

---

[4] This awe and affection for scarcely understood words is shared by other characters: in *La pata de la raposa*, Don Menardo, the ignorant *indiano*, is fond of the word "higiénico" which speaks to him of all good things; Don Leoncio, "se había encariñado con la palabra 'prematuro', bien que no alcanzase del todo su valor exacto; pero se le antojaba que contenía poder suasorio incontrovertible y vaga amenaza catastrófica" (*Luna*, p. 16).

valent terms. In the first group are words that simultaneously refer to several things or ideas: "Boscoso; adula, o como otros vulgares dicen, alude al boscan, que es una piel, al bosque o monte, porque hago botas de monte y al oso, porque se engrasa el material con unto de oso. Equitativo; porque hago botas de montar, o sea, de equitación, porque están hechas sobre seguro, como en la Equitativa, y porque la ciencia zapateresca ignora las cláusulas políticas" (p. 42). In the second group are words which Belarmino redefines to accord with their obvious homophonic implications. Thus "intuición" derives from the familiar pronoun "tú": "Dominio y familiaridad con un asunto. Vale tanto como tratar de tú" (p. 196); "lente" and "ente" are fused by virtue of a perspectivistic theory of consciousness — and also by reference to a famous cliché — "Lente-Ente. Todo es según el color del cristal con que se mira" (*loc. cit.*); "macilento" means "violento y contundente, como quien acomete con una maza" (p. 196); "escolástico" is one who "sigue opiniones ajenas, como la cola" (p. 195); "escorbútico" is "pesimista. Viene de cuervo" (p. 196). In two cases the definition shows Belarmino's relativistic scorn for dogma: "sistema" is "testarudez, obstinación. Refiérese a los que andan a vueltas con el mismo tema; si es tema" (p. 197), and "postema" is "sistema, teoría; tumor muerto que se forma dentro del cuerpo vivo" (p. 196). In some cases a mispronunciation or metathesis may disclose unsuspected significance: Belarmino says that "aludir es el dicho vulgar, el material tosco. Adular es la forma confeccionada. La alusión es siempre adulación" (p. 39).[5] Since these remodeled terms always retain the burden of their original sense, they reveal — as did the medieval etymologies, which were also derived by chance homophony — mysterious connections and correspondences.

Belarmino's language grows, as does all language, by metaphorical extension. Analogy may lead to simple replacement of one word by another: "joroba" is "responsabilidad, porque abulta, pesa y estorba;" "indumentario" is "lo externo y superficial;"

---

[5] Belarmino is not the only character to ferret out unlikely correlations; Apolonio also invents etymologies: "un monstruo de esos que llaman gárgolas, porque vomitan la lluvia con un ruido peculiar, de donde viene la frase hacer gárgaras" (p. 97).

because naming is the only true mode of congnition, "parafrasear" stands for "comprender;" many substitutions are quite obviously based on fixed formulae of thought: the vanity of the world makes "globo" replace "vanidad" and "Grecia," "sabiduría." The synonym may be the consequence of both metaphor and aural approximation: "sabio" is converted into "sapo" because "la sabiduría se adquiere mediante el éxtasis. El sapo es símbolo del éxtasis" (p. 197), a transformation that permits the author a sly attack: "Pues es un enormísimo sapo, mucho más grande aún que Salmerón" (p. 110). [6] The association may be imaginative, as in the case of the camel gradually transmogrified into "ministro de la Corona" (p. 87), [7] or analytical: "regar" means "visión de unidad, abarca con la mirada" because, if things exist only for a perceiving "Inteleto," conscious consideration refreshes and gives life to them, just as water gives life to the barren field (p. 196). But although language normally has a double function — a generalizing one that groups like things under the same label and a particularizing one that limits the inclusiveness of each term — Belarmino develops only the first. Advancing by poetic or logical comparisons, he attempts to tie together the most disconnected entities; he believes that metaphorical distention can ultimately lay bare the underlying unity of reality. The goal of his philosophy is one totally expressive word that will encompass the entire universe

---

[6] Charles Leighton (*op. cit.*) believes that Belarmino is a parody of the Krausists, who often committed stylistic outrages (see Juan López Morillas, *El krausismo español*, México, 1956, p. 51). One might also find an ironic version of Krausist ideals in Don Guillén's social theories (pp. 164-65). But one should also keep in mind that Pérez de Ayala agrees with certain presuppositions of those intellectual reformers: the belief in an ultimate harmony of the universe and the denial of the existence of evil (what is called evil is a temporary blindness, the result of a limited view of reality); he also shares with them a tendency to formulate rationalistic thought in religious terms (López Morillas, pp. 31, 37, and 84).

[7] *Camello*, decía el cosmos —es decir, el diccionario—; y Belarmino veía, en efecto, brotar de la página el dicho cuadrúpedo rumiante, aunque muy mermado de proporciones, y salir andando despaciosamente por el piso; pero a los pocos pasos, el perfil de la bestia, ya de suyo sinuoso, se deformaba más todavía, evolucionaba, se transformaba; el animal se ponía en dos pies, aparecía vestido con uniforme; la cabeza, sin perder la expresión primitiva, tomaba rasgos humanos; las jorobas se convertían en alforjas, que colgaban al pecho y espalda, y de una de las bolsas salía un gran cartapacio... Camello, de allí en adelante, significaría para él, ministro de la Corona (p. 87).

of thought: "La cuestión de la filosofía está en buscar una palabra que lo diga todo cuando nos da la gana" (p. 68) — a single, enormously ambiguous word to express the whole of reality.

This ideal is a mystical one and Belarmino, freeing words from the prison of common usage, feels "una manera de placer místico, un modo de comunicación directa con lo absoluto e íntima percepción de la esencia de las cosas" (p. 87). [8] He strives for a completely inclusive grasp of the world that lies beyond the particularizing and divisive realm of speech. By conciliating and absorbing semantic differences, he would void the world of diversity and contrast. His actual vocabulary imitates complexity, exposing in each concept a plurality of perspectives; but his ideal, the inconceivable condensation of all perspectives into a single term, would reduce complexity to unity. A total view would replace numberless relative viewpoints — and language would disappear. Thus, while Belarmino develops in practice and in theory the intuition of multiple realities, his search for a solitary all-meaningful word is a reversed reflection of the relativistic theme.

The Language of the Narrator

The polyglot speech of the characters derives from the jumbled conglomeration of human perspectives. The narrator's speech supplements the chorus of mixed voices and suggests, in its variety, multiple stylistic systems. Pérez de Ayala pieces together a linguistic mosaic, an anthology of verbal forms each one of which stands for a distinct point of view; he parodies classic diction, latinizes his prose (the omission of the definite article, certain rhetorical figures), molds Spanish to a foreign syntax, uses archaisms as well as words and phrases from regional dialects, popular

---

[8] The shoemaker's linguistics is also an esthetic creation. Don Guillén had observed this artistic inclination: "Él decía profesar la filosofía pero yo digo que tenía mucho de poeta" (p. 152). When Belarmino insists that the true understanding of an object is a dynamic gesture that brings into existence a new word, he is really describing the poetic act. "Cuando un hombre llama árbol a un árbol, porque ha oído llamar así, ese hombre no conoce el árbol ni sabe lo que dice, si conociese el árbol, lo hubiera creado él mismo, le hubiera dado un nuevo nombre" (pp. 86-87).

expressions, and slang. He shows the distance between his own and a character's vocabulary when he interrupts a train of thought to make a lexical correction:

> El propio Vespasiano, en su facha, maneras y conducta, era evasivo, resbaladizo, escurridizo, seductor, como una sierpe irisada. (A poseer Herminia algún rudimento de latín... en vez de aplicar a Vespasiano estos cuatro calificativos, se hubiera servido de una palabra que los resume a todos: lúbrico. (*Tigre*, pp. 242-243).

Or, by juxtaposing two deficient, banal modes of expression, he indicates his ironic superiority. [9]

In *Belarmino y Apolonio*, the linguistic theme is part of the novel's subject, but in other fictions it is elaborated through the structure: plot follows the hints of certain words and phrases. For Pérez de Ayala language is not an independent system that parallels perception, recording and translating data already completed outside the mind, but an interpretive tool, a precondition of conscious experience. Since abstraction and conceptualization (*gestalt* formation) cannot be separated from their symbolic frame, the known world is a verbal one, a universe already organized by conventional formulae. Therefore, the confusions traceable to language are an unavoidable and permanent part of human existence. Pérez de Ayala often dramatizes the duality inherent in the interpenetration of the real and the verbal (separable only in theoretical analysis, never in actuality) by demonstrating the way words body forth events and influence their course; he permits words to step out of the novel or story to direct and orchestrate the movements of the plot.

We have noted the use of ironic title puns (*La caída de los Limones*) and of proper names to create a symbolic situation ("El profesor auxiliar"). In another story, "Exodo," the revelation and denouement depend en Pepón's literal interpretation of his master's

---

[9] "A don Leoncio algunas palabras de María Egipcíaca (goloso, pescuezo, erisipela) le sentaban malísimamente. ¿Por qué no hablaría María Egipcíaca el lenguaje depurado y lindo de Micaela?
—Mujer; ese rojo encendido te agracia. Ahora sí que se puede decir de tus labios que son como pétalos de clavel fragante.
—Dirás que tengo el hocico como un tomate. (*Trabajos*, p. 145.)

rhetorical question ("¿Tú creías acaso, excelente Pepón, que ese lobezno era mi hijo?"). But it is in the two-part novel *Tigre Juan* and *El curandero de su honra* that Pérez de Ayala most thoroughly exploits language as a structural device: the climatic scenes are articulated by certain key terms so that the action seems to be a dramatic display of the words themselves.

In *Tigre Juan*, the protagonist tries to ward off the painful memories of his past (his wife's supposed infidelity and his own vengeance) by hiding behind a false and prejudiced picture of the world. The story (beginning after a series of illustrative scenes in a long exposition that takes up most of the section titled *Adagio*) traces his sudden enlightenment, the complete transformation of his view of the past and the consequent re-awakening of love (to which he is, however, blind). The revelation scene that climaxes the *Adagio* is almost a structural pun; a single word suggests all the images, each of which is like a strand unraveled from the rope of a common meaning. The several visions that present themselves to the *curandero* substantialize its diverse connotations. Tigre Juan has just read a letter from the wife of the army officer in whose home, years before, he had served as an orderly; as his past abruptly crashes back upon him he exclaims: "¡La Apoclipsi!!" (p. 155). The moment of the hero's revelation is called just that, and the following pages work it out in graphic detail; the various dramatic scenes are united by a common eschatological theme.

The doomsday vision begins with the letter, each of whose words sounds within the *curandero's* skull like "un trompetazo del Juicio Final" (they are also "seres vivos o resucitados," *loc, cit.*) next the spectral restoration of events confronts him as a menacing presence: "Su propio pasado, que Tigre Juan suponía abolido, se restauraba íntegro, cuajado en una eternidad de infierno, al conjuro de la generala Semprum, sacerdotisa de Belcebú." (*loc. cit.*). Just as the Last Judgement ends the dream of earthly life, the *curandero's* private apocalypse is the brusque awakening of a somnambulist, the break-down of a false, chimerical existence. Pérez de Ayala, here as elsewhere, ironically rewrites Christian tradition, reducing the grand theme of the vanity of worldy concerns to a minuscule, personalized version: the character's past stands in place of the whole "mundo falso" and the resurrection of the flesh is presented as the acute, almost physical recall of his youthful person:

> Era, para él, como el derrumbamiento y catástrofe de un mundo falso, perecedero, mundo de apariencias vanas, por él mismo fabricado, en el cual vivía adormido, trasvolado en un duermevela, tomando por realidades tangibles los sueños, de inmaterial urdimbre. Era ahora el instante de la resurrección de la carne, de su carne de mocedad, apasionada, dolorosa, ciega (p. 167).

Figures in this small apocalypse are grotesque and ludicrous:

> Y así como en el día del Juicio Final, en la gran zarabanda postrera de la vida y danza uinversal de la muerte, lo grotesco se abrazará con lo horrible, así también Tigre Juan, ante tantas memorias, ahora actuales, que le espantaban, fijó acaso la atención en un pormenor bufonesco. La capitana Semprún, con la bata entreabierta, camisa violeta y medias de pintas... le decía "Mis dos hijas mellizas nacieron a los siete u ocho meses después de tú haber salido de nuestra casa" (pp. 167-68).

Tigre Juan watches his own memories as if they were episodes in a staged drama: the general's wife is suddenly supplanted by another visualized bit of the past. "No siguió pensando en ella, porque se le antepuso, en el campo de la imaginaria contemplación, otro trozo de realidad trágica. Sentíase de nuevo estrangulando a Engracia, a quien idolatraba" (p. 168). Viewing the parade of events in consciousness like a spectator in the theater, he finally discovers Engracia's innocence (p. 169).

The *curandero* anxiously wonders if there can ever be salvation for him, not from the eternal fires of hell, but from the torments of his own conscience. That night, at Doña Marica's *tertulia*, his perception of well-known friends becomes momentarily hallucinatory: he sees them as masked skeletons jerked about in a macabre Judgement Day dance:

> Así Gamborena como doña Marica se le ofrecían bajo una óptica novísima y extraña, como si él y ellos estuvieran en el limbo o en el Valle de Josafat. Eran dos esqueletos, vestidos de máscara, que bailaban por resorte y emitían una risa artificial y rechinante (p. 179).

For the first time he notices that Herminia looks exactly like Engracia (p. 181). Half delirious, he is taken home muttering about "¡La Apocalipsi! ¡La resurrección de la carne!" (182); the *Adagio* ends with words whose import has shifted from the resucitation of the past to the reincarnation of a loved woman. Tigre Juan's exclamation thirty pages earlier has been discursively analyzed, its diverse implications lined up and illustrated in dramatic scenes: we see his past personified and resurrected, the crumbling of an illusory present, the revelation of Engracia's innocence, the metamorphosis of real people into grotesque mummers in an apocalyptic farce, and the raising of the dead in a chance resemblance. A metaphor patterns the novel's climax.

In the penultimate scene of the last section (*Presto*), the linguistic theme takes a slightly different form; instead of motivating the action through significant terms, the author sets up an almost formal debate between Iluminada and Herminia; their dialogue is a *conceptistic* play upon the word "querer" in its two sets of meaning, to will or want and to love. Iluminada tries to convince Herminia that she loves Tigre Juan, but the young woman turns those arguments about in such a way as to expose the kernel of self-interest in the widow's efforts:

> (Iluminada) —¡Qué mejor querer que querer para otros lo que uno para sí quisiera! Te quiero bien.
> —No señora —murmuró Herminia...— no me quiere bien. Querer para otros lo mismo que para sí, es ir contra el querer de los demás. Así quieren las personas mayores, que como ya no pueden querer, porque no pueden conseguir, sólo quieren obligar a los otros a que quieran sin querer...; los jóvenes no podemos querer sin querer, ni dejar de querer queriendo.
>
> * * *
>
> (Iluminada) —No poder querer sin querer, ni renunciar al querer queriendo, son imposibles (pp. 232-33).

Referring to one of the novel's central themes, the inseparability of illusion and happiness, the two women adroitly combine antithetical concepts: (Herminia) "El gusto que la mentira me da no es mentira... sino que es verdad, verdad; la única verdad amable" (p. 236); (Iluminada) "Es mentira que la felicidad exista; pero la ilusión de felicidad es felicidad verdadera" (p. 237).

Tigre Juan and *El curandero de su honra* progress from the obfuscations of the characters to a declaration of man's need for consoling fictions; in the expression of both topics the key words are the same — deceit, illusion, "engaño," "ilusión," but their affective connotations vary. The conclusion of the second volume, in which the protagonist envisions all life as a vast illusory scene in the mind of an unknown, hidden dreamer ("la vida es sueño"), is the final development and natural consequence of the thematic coupling of "engaño" and "ilusión." The actualization of these multifaceted concepts reaches its greatest complexity in the climactic *Adagio* of *El curandero*, where ideas are given almost tangible form. The text, which tells what happens to Tigre Juan and Herminia during their separation (a period of about twenty four hours) is divided into two columns representing the parallel course of two independent actions. According to the narrator's explanation, the lives of husband and wife had become so fused that each is included within the being of the other; their partial existences can be grasped only from that imaginary vantage point where both can be viewed at once. Although the occurrences in the two columns are approximately simultaneous, the device is not so much an attempt to synchronize different narrative episodes (it does do this to a certain extent) as to show, through a series of cross-column and vertical word-plays, the relations, oppositions, counterparts, and coincidences between the two lives. The titles of the novel's parts are musical tempos (Adagio, Presto, Codal), and in this section Pérez de Ayala gives a literary version of antiphonal composition on the leitmotifs of deception, revelation, and understanding. [10]

---

[10] Leon Livingstone, in "Interior Duplication and the Problem of Form in the Spanish Novel," *PMLA*, LXIII (1958), 405, has written that the two parallel columns are "intended to be read simultaneously" and judges the passage an example of attempted depth representation in the novel: "The attempt to replace the successive parade of images in two-dimensional description with the fusion of synchronical perspective in the experiment reveals the supreme difficulty of the presentation of depth in the novel, for the attempt is a brilliant failure. The reader cannot possibly absorb two columns at the same time and is thus forced to submit to chronological alternation in spite of the device." As I have noted in the last chapter, Li-

The columns cannot be taken in at one time, but if we read across them, we discover that a word or an idea bounces back and forth from one to the other, acquiring new shades of intent and disclosing inner antitheses; through this contrivance, reminiscent of stichomythic verse, the characters, unwittingly engage in a dialogue. The action, moving to the measure of reverberating words and phrases, receives yet another dimension in descriptions that illustrate it with visual symbols.

The passage opens with the discussion and realization of the multiple senses of "perder" (to lose, to ruin) and "querer". The column dealing with Tigre Juan tells of his fear of losing Herminia ("la posibilidad de perder a Herminia", p. 49) at the very moment that she, having pursued Vespasiano and joined him in the train to Regium, uses the word in quite a different way ("Caída, perdida estoy para siempre", (*loc. cit.*), Herminia joins "perder" with "querer" meaning "to will" when she insists that her "perdición" is the result of a determination of will ("no por mi gusto. Sí por mi voluntad", *loc. cit.*) while Vespasiano, with private and cynical interest, links freedom and true love (by freedom he means that neither he nor Herminia should make any claims upon the other — he proposes being her lover without the unpleasantness of an open break with Tigre Juan). Herminia responds that precisely because love permits no bonds, she has broken all ties and abandoned the home where she was "soberana" (p. 50). Like a person who begins to hum a tune heard he knows not where, Tigre Juan, in the other column, picks up the themes of freedom and will ("voluntad" and "querer") and brings them together in the ideal of free will, "albedrío" (A mí me concediste albedrío Señor, ¿De qué me sirve la libertad... si pensar no es lograr ni querer es poder?", (*loc. cit.*), "albedrío" which he has laid at the feet of the woman he reveres as "soberano" (*loc. cit.*). Just when Vespasiano restricts "querer" to sexual desire ("te quiero apasionadamente y te deseo, te deseo con angustia", p. 51) the other significance of "perder" suddenly occurs to the *curandero* ("¿Has pensado, de ligero, que la muerte no es el único modo de perderla?" (*loc. cit.*)

---

vingstone's concept of depth is based on an erroneous transfer of terms from Amaranto's metaphor. Nevertheless, the parallel columns do have a certain simultaneous effect because the reader, going down one side, cannot help but be aware of the other: he coordinates the two in his memory.

reminding him of the now dread honor code which, if obeyed to the exaction of vengence would entirely destroy him ("estás perdido sin remisión", p. 52). Rather than lose her in death, he prays that she deceive him and that he be blinded to her guilt ("sea yo antes burlado, con tal que ella viva... Ciégame si me burla", *loc. cit.*; this would be a reversal of his blindness to Engracia's innocence). In the meantime Herminia meditates on Vespasiano's egoistic notion of "libertad". The unraveling of the different semantic strands in "perder" and "querer" is then suspended, for Tigre Juan's inner conflict gives way to an external and humorous incident —the peasant beating his wife and the *curandero's* attempts to rescue her; this farcical anecdote, unconnected with the plot, relates to it in theme alone— it is a comic development of the honor motif.

The interweaving of action, motif, and word continues, making a kind of chiaroscuro tapestry that depicts first the characters' blindness to the true meaning of love and then their enlightenment, which takes place, appropriately enough, on Saint John's night. Don Sincerato, who lies dying in his asylum for deaf-mutes initiates (in Tigre Juan's column) the blindness-enlightenment motif: he sees his imminent ascension to heaven prefigured in the magical practices of the night; the light of the bonfires on all the hilltops is magnified into an other-worldly refulgence. "Noche de San Juan. Rosada celestial sobre los prados. Todas las flores se abren. Olor a paraíso... Cuantas hogueras rojas; aquí, allí, acullá, más allá. Toda la tierra es claridad. El Dios de la luz vence al príncipe de las tinieblas" (p. 71). His words allude to and forecast Tigre Juan's transformation, and that of all the other lovers — Colás and Carmina, Carmen and Lino. The author uses both the ancient pagan rites of Midsummer, Christian mythology, and the old priest's humble faith for their expressive and symbolic value. Herminia laments that her love for her husband was blind (p. 74), and Colás says to Carmina, "Bendita sea tu divina sinceridad, luz inmaculada que penetra los últimos recovecos del alma y disipa las sombras más insidiosas" (p. 79). As if on the cue of certain words (blindness-clarity, "ceguera-claridad") and their visual correlates in the customs of St. John's night ("se abrían las grandes amapolas de las hogueras", p. 78), the narrator works out the topics of misunderstanding and illumination, welding the parallel columns into a dense mesh of inseparable components. Action, descriptions, and wordplays fit so neatly together that the reader takes a phrase from one column, an image from the other, a scene here, a speech there, and braids the two threads into a single chain. Back and forth between the columns the author reiterates references to sights, sounds, and smells — the great fires, the piercing cries of the *ijujú*, the choruses of young men and young women, the odors of mint and elder blossom. Within the same column, pictorial image links with simile, disclosing new associative possibilities (the fire stands not only for amorous enlightenment but also for the raging jealousy of Tigre Juan: "Oyendo a Tigre Juan bramar a la manera del fuego cuando acelera su extincción, Nachín sonreía... pensando: 'bufa, bufa, que cuando más bufes, más aina el fuego será humo y el humo será nada'... Pululaban ya las hogueras. Parecía que el fuego oprimido en el seno del orbe... estallaba en una erupción de menudos cráteres", p. 78).

Then a new, but closely related theme begins — "engaño", another multifaceted concept (deceit, trickery, marital infidelity, self-deception, illusion) whose different meanings are spread out in the dialogue and action. Herminia, accompanied by Carmen and Lino, comes upon, in the town of Mañas (cunning, craftiness), Carmina and Colás who are entertaining the townsfolk with a mind-reading performance, accomplished by means of certain clever deceits. But no sooner does the narrator introduce "engaño" than he seems to hold it in temporary abeyance in order to show the lovers, against a sensory backdrop of songs, chants, and magical deeds, embracing and declaring their love. The amorous concord they exemplify (evident in the phonic coalescence of their names: Carmen la del Molino, Lino, Carmina, Colás) is viewed by Tigre Juan (in the other column) with the detachment of one who sees *sub specie aeterni* and dissolves reality into evanescent dream; thus "amor" and "ilusión" prepare for the reintroduction of "engaño". The dissociation between Tigre Juan, spectator, and the world of love, is manifest not only in what he says but in the theatrical frame of his words: at this point dialogue adopts a play-format:

Tigre Juan... contemplaba ahora, sub specie aeterni, la realidad como un sueño evanescente. Como si de sus ojos emanase un agente corrosivo, Tigre Juan, mirando al mundo exterior, percibía que, involucrados unos en otros los elementos, el mundo se desintegraba y fluía, fluía, con fugitivas mudanzas...

Nachín de Nacha. Noche de encantos. Como fierro e imán, apégase lo más enemigo, que son home y muyer. ¡Pobrinos! Con los primeros rayinos del sol, desfarase el encanto. Todo fuxe.

Era la mágica noche de los enamorados. Todas las criaturas mortales, acoplados, se eternizaban, por el amor. Herminia se veía tan sola...

Tigre Juan. Lo fugitivo es lo eterno. Sí: todo cambia, huye, se aleja de mí. Yo permanezco a solas... (p. 80).

Love is invoked as both a magical delusion and a constant principle: the ephemeral and the eternal merge. The topic of "engaño", always hovering nearby, then reappears in the right-hand column as Colás and Carmina explain their repertory of tricks, Herminia reproaches them for deceiving others, and Colás defends himself with the claim that this harmless "engaño" hurts none and amuses all. Then, slightly twisting and enlarging the meaning of the word, he says that "la vida está entretejida de sútiles engaños" (p. 82). At this moment, in the opposite column Nachín de Nacha's rustic superstitions ("Veo pantasmas. Homes y muyes abrazándose. Pantasmas. Oigo las tarramelas de la culiebra. Oigo los blincos del trasgo y la risada del diablo burlón", pp. 81-82) set the stage for the *curandero's* "engaño" of the senses: the appearance of Engracia's ghost, who reminds us of still another meaning when she tells her husband, "No te engañé. Te engañaste" (Joining both meanings Tigre Juan asks, "¿Y ahora, me engaño también?"). Meanwhile Colás asserts that love is the only truth in a deceptive world and Carmen, thinking of women "engañadas por el amor", argues that "el amor es también un engaño" (p. 82). Throughout the dialogue and scenic presentation the narrator pursues the examination of the various denotations and connotations of "engaño", concluding with this punning exchange of paradoxes:

—De todas suertes, la dicha o la desdicha que este gran engaño del amor ocasiona son las únicas verdades de la vida— dijo Colás.
—Por miedo a su desdicha, yo quisiera desengañarme y desengañarle— dijo Carmen, la del molino.
—No parece sino que padece usted un engaño penoso (p. 83).

We noted that the word-play preceding the conclusion of *Tigre Juan* opened with a discussion of the ambivalences of the word "querer" and closed with Iluminada's exaltation of "mentira-ilusión"; the sequence here is similar, beginning with "perder" and "querer" and ending with the transformation of "engaño" from despised deceit into life-sustaining illusion. The last shift in import and value recapitulates the whole of the story — from Tigre Juan's sudden "desengaño" about his wife's imagined adultery ("engaño") to the equation of "engaño" and "ilusión".

As if applying a refracting prism to his expressive medium, the author compels each linguistic element to give up all of its significations. Like the shoemaker-philosopher, he turns each word this way and that, elucidates semantic ties, spreads out and illustrates its numerous allusions and implications, and then jumbles them back together; on the resulting ambiguity he builds his narrative. The linguistic perspectivism that underlies the humor of *Belarmino y Apolonio* becomes the basis of contrapuntal composition in *Tigre Juan* and *El curandero de su honra*. The first novel is the comic destruction of man's intellectual attempts to submit the world to a coherent scheme, and its word plays and puns suggest that reality, as well as its symbolic representation in language, is unstable and fundamentally confounding. The second novel is an affirmation of the amorous harmony that Pérez de Ayala sees as the essence of ultimate reality, and its conceptistic devices would seem to point to that merging of antitheses which is the verbal counterpart of an ordered universe.

Chapter IV

REALITY AND ART

In all his fictions, Pérez de Ayala attends to the problem of the artist creating. The novelist as character in the early autobiographical works is replaced in his mature period by the novelist as a conspicuous fabricator who may not appear within the story himself (though he is by no means adverse to such intrusions) but who none the less makes himself a focal object. His machinations, his intellectual preoccupations, and his concept of the novel persistently obtrude. We have examined some of his techniques for dealing with a world of numerous fragmented perspectives ordered and held together by the author's own attitudes: as narrator he shifts between a subjective and an objective treatment; as humorist he establishes his ironic superiority by proliferating conflicting systems of ideas; in the manipulation of language, he brings us even closer to his own artistic contrivances, to his novelist's work room. The interdependence of words and experience leads to the broader theme of the interpenetrating realms of art and reality: just as the word is the frame of perception, the determinant and augur of events, so too the work of literature permeates life, reproducing itself in people and situations and giving intelligible form to unpatterned events. The subject of aesthetic conversion, of life made into literature, is ultimately related to Pérez de Ayala's conception of the novel as a *concordia discors*, a picture of total reality in which warring impulses and values fall into place as the necessary components of a perfect design.

The Characters Transform Life into Art

In certain respects Pérez de Ayala has made his fictional creatures in his own image; with him they share a tendency to convert lived reality into the recollection of some well-known work of art. The protagonist of *La pata de la raposa*, a young painter, decides to abandon his artistic pursuits in order to free himself from the morbid self-consciousness that impedes a direct perception of the world; he sets out for the country to live in rustic animality. But the painter's habits have not left him: he cannot help but see, in the persons and tableaux of a village inn, replicas of famous works of art: "Un minero se levantó... le veía acercarse, con curiosidad desinteresada, *artística*. La lentitud, el movimiento..., su cráneo anguloso y su fortaleza torpe y bovina, hacían que Alberto imaginase tener ante sus ojos una escultura de Meunier, semoviente, viva" (p. 19); "Alberto se sentía en plena ingenuidad, frescura y barbarie de espíritu. Cuanto le rodeaba le producía el deleite de la *emoción estética* (p. 49); "El cuadro de la taberna... era Jordaens o Teniers... De vez en vez, a la luz de un relámpago, se encendía el paisaje con un resplandor azul intenso y violeta; y era la aparición subitánea de esas creaciones de Patinir... Una voz moza cantaba. Era un aire de austera melancolía labriega, como las romanzas de Grieg y de Rimski-Korsakof" (p. 50); another girl reminds him of "esas hembras pingües y fáciles... en las kermeses de Rubens (p. 50); "su falda... añil muy vivo... semejante a los añiles de Fra Angélico" (p. 51); "Erguíase su tronco con dignidad, como la Mnemosme, de Lysipo" (*loc. cit.*); her father "estaba cruzado de brazos, con el gesto socarrón y hierático del escriba egipcio que hay en el Museo del Louvre" (*loc. cit.*). Finally the character becomes aware that he is transmuting objects and people into artistic reproductions:

> He aquí que me apercibo a gozar por primera vez de las cosas como si hubieran sido creadas sólo para mí, y ¿qué ha sucedido? Que no veo con mis ojos ni oigo con mis oídos. La realidad permanece ajena y misteriosa para mí. Entre ella y yo se interponen las imágenes y las sensaciones expresadas por otros sentidos... ¿Soy un hombre o soy un portafolio de estampas? (pp. 52-53).

In varying degrees, all the characters view their surroundings and their own lives in terms of art. Frequently they find themselves actors playing assigned roles; reality is "el gran teatro del mundo." In *Troteras y danzaderas*, Alberto Díaz de Guzmán (hero of the previous novel), now an aspiring writer, likes to theorize about the drama. His belief that ethics and politics depend upon esthetic sensibility leads him to describe the political life of Spain in theatrical terms. "El espíritu de la raza a que pertenezco y la vida histórica de esta nación... ¿son trágicos o melodramáticos?: ¿Soy actor de coturno y persona, dignidad y decoro incorporado a la caudal tragedia humana, o soy fantocha en una farsa lacrimosa y grotesca?" (p. 119). This tendency to see life as drama leads to a severing of the critical consciousness from sentiment; one becomes a spectator of his own self: "—Todo consiste en meterse entre los bastidores de uno mismo, introspeccionarse, convertirse de actor en espectador y mirar del revés la liviandad y burda estofa de todos estos bastidores, bambalinas y tramoya del sentimiento humano" (pp. 244-45). In *Luna de miel, luna de hiel*, Urbano, brought back to his mother after his disastrous honeymoon, feels that he has been playing the lead in an incomprehensible comedy (p. 272). Don Cástulo Colera, usually "el eterno espectador" at one point discovers himself a personage in a tragic farce ("una tragedia bufa, que es un género despreciable, híbrido, en fin, romántico," *Luna*, p. 113). His reactions to life are usually literary: a given reality does not elicit his intervención, but rather propels him towards the investigation of its artistic representation; confronted with Urbano and Simona's absurd predicament, he wonders under what literary genre it might be classified: "¿Égloga, o tragedia? Nada, que me entrego. Converso soy al romanticismo. El amor es una cosa trágica y grotesca de consuno. Sin duda hay géneros literarios híbridos como hay animales híbridos" (p. 129). Even Urbano notices that his mentor is unable to perceive the world except through the mirror of art: "La naturaleza y el mundo y la vida ¿existen para usted fuera de los libros?" (p. 183).

Tigre Juan is one of the characters most obviously oriented toward the stage; it has shaped his notion of honor, affected his speech, and even predeterminado the means of his attempted suicide (*Curandero*, p. 101). A member of an amateur theatrical company, he plays with greatest pleasure the offended husband in Calderón's *comedias* (his favorite ones are *A secreto agravio, secreta venganza* and *El médico de su honra*). So hypnotized is he by the drama, that real emotional transport can only be compared to the effects of theatrical catharsis, as when he experiences "una manera de dichoso embobamiento, como ante una apoteosis escénica de gran aparato y tramoya" (*Tigre Juan*, p. 187). Life is sometimes as moving as art. Doña Mariquita takes advantage of his known weakness "apercibiéndose a escenificar un patatús de gran espectáculo" (p. 203).

The written word too bewitches these characters who live vicariously in fantastic worlds made out of bookish elements. In his dream-life, Don Cástulo imagines himself courting the Ionic and Corinthian courtesans of classical erotic literature.[1] Marco de Setiñano fancies himself a reincarnation of his favorite heroe (*Prometeo*); Apolonio's procedure is different: instead of inserting himself in an unreal world, he draws literary figures down into his humble shoemaker's environment: "Si nombraba a Ovidio o a Sófocles, era como si hubieran comido juntos pote gallego" (*Belarmino*, p. 69). All the characters in *Tigre Juan* and *El curandero de su honra* are dedicated to one or another author or literary genre. Tigre Juan can quote classical Spanish sources on the honor theme; Colás's romanticism is derived from a single book, *Werther* (p. 61); Doña Iluminada immerses herself in the ingenuous unreality of fairy tales and chivalry novels, occasionally transferring their values into her own experience: "Colás hizo lo mejor..., salir a realizar proezas por las siete partidas del orbe; cosa digna de un caballero andante, como no se ve ya en estos tiempos" (p. 136). Even those who may never have read a book

---

[1] Don Cástulo vivía dos vidas paralelas, autónomas y sin mutuo contacto entre sí; una vida real y una vida imaginaria. Los ratos de ocio y solaz los consumía en leer autores eróticos, griegos y latinos. Su imaginación estaba atiborrada de erotismo literario y vaporoso, que jamás se insertaba en la vida real, por falta de datos de los sentidos y puntos de referencia experimentales. Imaginariamente, andaba siempre lamentando, con epigramático aticismo, el desvío de alguna cortesana jónica, corintia o acaso beocia: Erisila, Prodicea, Melisa, Heliodora, Berenice. Algunas noches, acostado Urbano, don Cástulo decía que iba a tomar el aire. Era la coyuntura en que sus divagaciones imaginarias asumían corporeidad y acción. Perdíase en las callejuelas fuera de mano, y sentándose en el umbral de cualquiera mansión ignorada, supuesta vivienda de la desdeñosa cortesana de tanda, suspiraba con palabras de Calímaco. (*Luna*, pp. 46-47.)

live absorbed in fictions vulgarized in the *folletín* or in popular song. Adriana ("La triste Adriana") imagines chimerical melodramas in which she is always the tragic protagonist ("Poco a poco sin darse cuenta, halló que todas sus fantasías paraban en suponerse adúltera..., era por necesidad interior de un gran conflicto, de una gran congoja" (*Ombligo*, p. 86); as the story progresses, real events seem to imitate her day-dreams, and she finds it increasingly difficult to distinguish between the two. Tigre Juan's first wife, Engracia, sings flamenco *coplas* celebrating crimes of jealousy ("el fatal ayuntamiento de amor y muerte"), songs that not only presage her fate but reconcile her to it: "Con tales ingredientes de afinidad patética, se estaba fraguando la elegía roja, el drama" (*Tigre*, p. 161).

The Autonomous Character

The ironic narrator, who intrudes in the action and discusses the problems of his art with the reader, calls attention to his own activities and thereby attenuates the illusion of reality within the work. But if he breaks down the walls protecting the novel's inner consistency and verisimilitude, he does so in order to equate the limits of the fictitious world with those of our experienced one. With no barriers between story and life, the novelist is free to enter and leave as he pleases; as if in a curtainless theater, he can be seen pulling strings and pushing the stage properties around in full view of the audience. And by the same token, characters may step out and assert their independence, either by confronting the author (as in Unamuno's *Niebla*) or, less obtrusively, by taking a hand in the direction of the plot. In *Belarmino y Apolonio*, the zones of reality and fiction merge because the narrators, one a character, the other the author, can meet and converse: Don Guillén, in his long monologues directed to the first-person speaker, may be considered a co-narrator of the novel. Another fictional creature, the ghost of Don Amaranto, although doubly unreal by virtue of being a mere apparition in his author's memory, becomes autonomous when, allowing himself the liberty of addressing the novelist with the familiar *tú*, he undertakes to advise him on his craft (p. 28).

In *Tigre Juan* and *El curandero de su honra* one of the characters, Doña Iluminada, functions as a kind of assistant novelist, for to a great extent she engineers the loves of Tigre Juan and Herminia and of Colás and Carmina; it is as if she were writing the scenario whose outlines they unwittingly follow. Convinced that life can be made to reproduce the pattern of a romantic tale, she habitually thinks of her efforts as literary creation: "Lo leo en la blanca página de los destinos. Aquí entra mi misterio" (*Tigre*, p. 220). She has discovered the principle of unconscious imitation whereby a suggestion properly implanted determines a whole series of events.[2]

If reality is to be obedient to her design, the characters must be properly educated for their roles; they must be charmed by fantasy, won over by agreable if improbable fictions. The virtuous *celestina* notes with pleasure Herminia's susceptibility to a certain kind of literature:

—Te agradaría que la vida fuese como un cuento.
—Sí, señora.
—Apuesto que no has perdido afición a leer cuentos. O por mejor decir, a imaginarlos.

* * *

—Y aquellos que más te atraen son los cuentos de miedo y angustia, que al final todo se arregla a pedir de boca (*Tigre*, p. 237).

Sedulously she nurtures Carmina's imagination with fairy tales and chivalry novels (*Curandero*, p. 29) and depicts the absent Colás as "arquetipo de donceles y príncipe de amadores perfectos" (p. 31); in the girl's eyes she foresees and reads the very love story that she, Iluminada, is writing ("los ojos legibles de la niña donde

---

[2] Iluminada había verificado una curiosa experiencia. Comenzaba a canturrear, en voz apenas audible, los primeros compases de una canción. Callaba al pronto y aguardaba. A los pocos momentos, todos tarareaban por lo bajo, distraídamente la misma canción... Y pensaba la viudad: "quien siembra trigo, cosecha trigo; ...La simiente no se pierde jamás... el toque estriba en coger a las almas por sorpresa, cuando están ensimismadas (*Curandero*, p. 30.)

venía el futuro que ella deseaba," *Tigre*, p. 222). Carmina is the fabrication of her step-mother, modeled out of the substance of her soul; Iluminada loves by determination of the will, *through* another being, who might be called an amorous alter-ego ("La simiente que en ella he sembrado soy yo misma," (*Curandero*, p. 32).

When the love story seems headed for a disatrous conclusion, the widow assumes all the blame, for she is "la autora de todo" (*Curandero*, p. 73), sole contriver of the farce. In declaring her guilt, she evokes the classic Cervantine example of the deceptive boundaries between reality and art: "La adversidad se ceba en todos vosotros, y a mí, la autora de tanta tragedia, egoísta maese Pedro de este aflictivo retablo, monumento de nubes, tan presto levantado como venido al suelo..." (*Op. cit.*, p. 88). Doña Iluminada's guiding role in the construction of the double love story is mentioned here and there throughout the novel; the literary undertaking of one of the characters thus becomes a recurring motif in the narrative's composition. If the novelist seeks to impose an order upon life by transmuting it into fiction, Iluminada attempts the reverse, to turn fiction into life.

The Narrator Transforms Life into Art: Parody and Artistic Transposition

All literature is, of course, a transformation of reality, but Pérez de Ayala makes the transformation itself a conspicuous feature of the work, so that we see not only life converted into art but also this life-art conversion itself made into art. He constructs the work out of materials already formed and stylized.

We have noted two tendencies in this writer's thought, on the one hand a relativistic approach to knowledge and on the other, a metaphysical absolutism that envisions an ultimate harmony resulting from the balance of conflicting forces. His numerous devices for interchanging the roles of reality and literature are congruent with either tendency: artistic transpositions sometimes serve a detached and ironic relativism that, delighting in the shifting frontiers between what is and what is invented, exposes the illusory quality of all cultural fabrications; but they also can function as illustrations of that process whereby man can organize the chaotic flux of experience. In the first case the novelist's humor is as apt to undermine his own art as any other system; in the second, his art appears to congeal the diversity of life into a fixed design of contrasting parts.

Pérez de Ayala, the perspectivist and ironist, engages in literary, philosophical, and religious parody to depict that fall of the ideal or of the mythical which Ortega says is essential in the novelistic genre. In his first novel, *Tinieblas en las cumbres*, he produces an anthology of satires of various literary forms: a picaresque preface in which a penitent sinner pleads that the account of his waywardness may help to keep others on the path of virtue; a pseudo-erudite disquisition on the history of prostitution; an intercalated story whose chapter titles suggest the melodramatic episodes of the "novela erótica" ("Rosina nace y se desarrolla. Un hombre que tiene los ojos gordos la codicia bajamente," p. 57); and finally, a pastiche of mystic phraseology to describe Rosina's seduction.

Parodic fragments appear in many of his stories and novels. In the early collection, *Bajo el signo de Artemisa*, "Padre e hijo" is a reminiscence of the gothic tale, still further exaggerated in its farcical grotesqueness; "El anticristo" is called an "Ejemplo" (though its moral is quite distinct from that of any medieval apologue). An explicit topic of *Prometeo* is the degeneration of the myth, measured in the devolution from poetry to prose ("lo que en las edades épicas fue canto heroico, al son de la cítara, es ahora voz muda y gráfica... El aeda ha degenerado en novelador," p. 9), in the metamorphosis of Ulysses and Calypso into Juan Pérez and Federica Gómez, and in the corruption of the epic into village gossip ("Canta, oh diosa cominera de estos días plebeyos, diosa de la curiosidad impertinente y tedio fisgón... Canta o cuenta. ¡Oh diosa chismorrera y correveidile!", pp. 9-10). Belarmino Pinto is both a modern-day Sócrates (complete with a "demonio íntimo," his "Inteleto") and, in his linguistic theory, a *reductio ad absurdum* of certain early twentieth-century movements in philosophy and poetry. In *Tigre Juan* and *El curandero de su honra*, Pérez de Ayala reflects two archetypes of the Spanish Golden Age theater in the distorting mirror of burlesque — Juan Guerra, the would-be Calderonian avenger of honor, and

Vespasiano Cebón, an effeminate provincial Tenorio. The comic treatment of religious or classical themes may be limited to a laconic allusion, an ironic comparison of vulgar reality to a famous work of art: "Belarmino era cabalmente el remedo animado de San Francisco, de Luca de la Robbia... También Platón tenía las sienes anchas" (p. 143); "remedaba las imágenes de los santos que recibieron la gracia de los estigmas" (p. 199).

Pérez de Ayala persistently secularizes religious terminology and concepts, rendering them "a lo humano." The language of courtly love, adopted by the Spanish mystics of the sixteenth century, is reapplied to carnal passion (for example, Rosina's seduction in *Tinieblas*). He uses Christian myth and symbol in the arrangement of episodes in a love affair, as in the apocalypse passages of *Tigre Juan* or in the reunion of Angustias and Pedrito in *Belarmino y Apolonio*. To describe the latter scene, Don Guillén quotes the Breviary: "*in thesauro reposita*... el dracma extraviado ha sido repuesto en los tesoros del rey, y la perla luce nuevamente, sacada desde la tiniebla a la claridad" (p. 172).

Whereas parody is the deprecatory inclusion of cultural creations, artistic transpositions imply an affirmation of art; if parody pulls the revered down to the level of the ordinary, artistic transpositions elevate common things to what the writer must consider a more exalted region. But in Pérez de Ayala these transfers do not so much embellish the work (their function in Modernist prose) as they suggest the freezing of the instability and changeableness of life into a willed pattern. By situating the novelistic materials in a museum-like realm where masterworks of all periods co-exist in a timeless present, the author destroys the illusion of reality in favor of his own self-conscious esthetic order. The transformation of characters into figures from literary history is a device at the service of his objectifying, dehumanizing vision.

Many such transpositions are references to art inserted almost at random in the narrative: the garden of Doña Rosita's country house, "exquisito poema bucólico, compuesto en vivo" (*Luna*, p. 109); Simona sleeping "parecía... el Adonis dormido y marmóreo de la estatuaria griega" (*Trabajos*, p. 266) or, in the belvedere she is "oteando, como la hermana en el cuento de Barba Azul" (*Luna*, p. 109). The fairy tale is the source of several transmogrifications—the seven witch-like step sisters in *Trabajos* whose house encloses "un cuento triste de hadas" (p. 173) and the magic garden of the Limons in Guadalfranco (*Prometeo*). An allusion to sculpture, which converts the body into spatial form, may momentarily detain the actors in their movement: "El tiempo había detenido también su andadura... Todos permanecían en una estática relación trágica; grupo escultórico de un paso de Semana Santa, que perpetuase diferentes escorzos, inestables y patéticos" (*Curandero*, p. 96).

Pérez de Ayala sometimes utilizes certain dramatic situations or the general plot outline of a previous literary work. He may interpret a traditional story in a new way: "La triste Adriana" and "Artemisa" are modern re-workings of classical themes. In *Luna de miel, luna de hiel* and its sequel, *Los trabajos de Urbano y Simona*, literary echoes abound: the three primary classical inspirations are *Daphnis and Cloe*, Cervantes' development of the Byzantine novel, and the motif of the "educación del príncipe."[3] Longus's story of innocent lovers provides the novel's central situation, and even the characters are aware of the duplication (Cástulo says "Dafnis y Cloe, redivivos. *Nihil novum sub sole*," *Luna*, p. 98). Doña Micaela, the real author of this contemporary version, had attempted to impose on life, in the person of her son Urbano, an ideal of perfect purity. Urbano's tutor, Don Cástulo, compares her plan to the education of "los príncipes herederos" (p. 49), to the schemes of Plato and Calderón (p. 43); he imagines a fantasy about a youth who, by his father's decree, is brought up in a cave, isolated from all human contact, "e ideando estos caprichos, recordó el Segismundo de *La vida es sueño*" (p. 69). In the second volume, seventeenth-century topics become compositional motifs: Simona, imprisoned in a convent, is rescued in a scene that recalls the exploits of Don Juan; Urbano, who wants to reenact with Simona a *comedia* adventure, suggests that for their trip to Santander, she disguise herself as a boy because

---

[3] Rafael Cansinos Assens, in *La nueva literatura, 1917-1927* (Madrid, 1927), refers to this anthologizing inclination of Pérez de Ayala: "Ha acertado amalgamar en sus novelas más representantes, como *Los trabajos de Urbano y Simona* and *Tigre Juan*, varios instantes en la evolución del género y varias épocas del desarrollo del idioma... En cualquiera de las novelas grandes de Ayala encontramos resumida toda una historia literaria y gustamos sabores de múltiples obras magistrales" (pp. 107-108).

"en las comedias clásicas sucedía con frecuencia que las enamoradas viajaban disfrazadas de hombre" (p. 279).

The novel fails, however, properly to conjoin fantasy and reality, because it forces a marriage of incompatible parts: an unrealistic, purely imaginary premise is developed in a realistically pictured environment of middle-class provincial Spain — and apparently the author's intent is neither satirical nor allegorical. Instead of parodying the Daphnis and Cloe fable (and thereby showing the imposibility of the myth), or using it as a symbolic point of reference in an allegory (in which case the plot could be more or less independent of the known world), he has attempted a modern-dress production.[4] And he feels compelled to justify his improbable tale by recurring to an argument about a human and poetic truth that is more true than mere historical fact; through Don Cástulo he pleads his own case with the reader:

> Os estoy viendo reir, con vuestra risa espesa. Os reís de la tragedia, como os reís de la mitología. Los mitos los juzgáis inverosímiles y los calificáis de cuentos de viejas. Lo que no comprendéis, decretáis que no existe. Si supierais de Antígona, diríais que no es verosímil, y que por lo tanto no existió. Si supierais de Micaela, de Urbano, de Simona, diríais que son inverosímiles y que por lo tanto no existen. Yo, el más inverosímil de todos, soy el que menos existo. Pues sí, a pesar del vulgo, a pesar de vosotros, existo. Aquí me tenéis contra toda lógica y verosimilitud" (*Trabajos*, p. 13).

This is not the autonomous character defying the reader but the author himself defending his incongruous concoction. Because Pérez de Ayala here rendered myth as actuality, the personages and setting do not take on a mythical aura, as they might have done

---

[4] Nor does he create a fantastic tale, for in that genre, impossible events are effectively situated among ordinary experience in one of two ways: either the unreal nucleus contaminates the whole world of the fiction and even the real world of the reader with a hallucinatory quality (as in Borges or Kafka), or the fantastic nature of the story is not made explicit but only alluded to, so that the occurrences would allow a simple realistic (often psychological) explanation — an explanation which would, however, destroy their inner, magical probability (a medieval example and a modern one: Juan Manuel's "Don Illán y el deán de Santiago" and Adolfo Bioy Casares's *El sueño de los héroes*).

in a more suggestive, symbolic treatment. Since the myth is by nature refractory to literal interpretation, the two elements remain inconsonant and jarring.

Artistic entities incorporated into the narrative may be structurally represented through the combination of heterogeneous form —story, essay, poetry, drama. We have remarked the use of essay-like discourses to frame the plot of a novel or story. In the three "novelas poemáticas" (*Proemteo, Luz de domingo,* and *La caída de los Limones*)—as well as in one volume of short stories, *El ombligo del mundo*—the author prefaces chapters with poems, usually in traditional or archaic meters that, by their evocation of the epic or the medieval lyric, give a period quality to the work and set it apart from contemporary reality (he has compared them to the illuminated capitals in medieval manuscripts, *Poesías completas,* p. 16). These verses provide different perspectives on the action: some are didactic pieces in which the author states the moral of the story (those of "La triste Adriana," "Clib," and several of the poems in *Prometeo*). Others are like poetic illustrations which lyrically portend the theme to be pursued in prose (for example, en *Luz de domingo,* the introductory poem on the delights of "la vida retirada," or the one that precedes "Don Rodrigo y don Recaredo") or divulge a part of the action (the blind man's song in *Luz*). Most of them are miniature allegorical versions of the prose plot, showing parallel instances and foreshadowing the turns of events. This anticipatory function prevents the build-up of suspense because it shatters a dynamic sequence into semi-isolated episodes whose climactic moments have been previously announced; the novels (especially *Luz*) thereby acquire a ballad-like form, that of a well-known epic condensed to the lyrically expressed scenes of most intense drama.

The poems also offer disconsonant perspectives within the novel in *Luz de domingo,* the rape of Balbina by the seven Becerril brothers feudal lords of the region, is foretold by the prefatory citation from the *Poema del Cid* ("¡Quál ventura serie esta, si ploguiese al Creador, que assomase esora el Cid Campeador!"), later referred to in the malicious verses of a blind ballad singer, and finally chronicled by one of the characters in a sarcastic and lascivious tale ("un literato provinciano refería la afrenta de la pomarada de la hermite, no a la manera castellana, del poema del

Cid, sino contrahaciendo el estilo irónico y lascivo de Boccacio", *Prometeo*, p. 133). A tragic event passes through the prismatic refractions of different literary genres, the epic, the street song, the bawdy tale.

The inclusion of dramatic fragments in the narration is a common expedient in these fictions. With the interpolation of a theatrical scene, the story-teller momentarily abandons his traditional role of commentator in order to imitate the dramatist's direct mode of composition: speeches stand alone without explanatory introductions like "he said," and description takes the form of parenthetical stage directions. Because a play presents events in the present, as they happen, and without the mediation of a narrator, such shifts might be expected to heighten the immediacy and poignancy of the passage (as they do in Melville's *Moby Dick*, for instance). But in Pérez de Ayala quite the contrary occurs; far from becoming more life-like, the action is derealized, for to evoke staged drama is to suggest the transmutation of reality into its theatrical representation. The play-like sections are static interludes that, instead of intensifying the drama, interrupt and delay its unfolding. The technique is a large-scale artistic transposition. Pérez de Ayala used it in early stories and in the later novels: we have mentioned the two interpolations of play-format in "Exodo" and the way they contribute to the abstract stylization of the work ("Exodo" and its sequel "Padre e hijo" are in their methodical deformations and exaggerations, similar to Valle-Inclán's "comedias bárbaras"). In *A. M. D. G.* the chapter titled "Consejo de pastores" (pp. 99-102) is dialogue with stage directions, a non-dramatic, exemplary passage, as is a later scene in which the author creates the stage atmosphere by inserting descriptive material parenthetically into the speeches of the interlocutors: "(Aquí la voz del Padre Olano se hace recia y tonante. Telva simula suspirar)" (p. 216). [5] In the last chapter of *Belarmino y Apolonio* ("Sub specie aeterni"), action gives way to a chorus of stock types ("el indiano", "el borracho", "el glotón", "el usurero", etc.) gathered together in a dance of death review.

---

[5] Most of the tableaux of this novel are independent; there is no line of developing plot but only a succession of situations and incidents that exemplify various horrors of Jesuit education. The book has no real dramatic structure.

Another theatrical device is the arrangement of characters into a motionless tableau in which the emotional import is conveyed not in dialogue but in significant and stilted gestures and in the spatial disposition of persons and objects. The death of Doña Rosita in *Los trabajos* is a visual and auditory representation in which graphic details and the reiteration of a locative phrase ("allí estaba") spatialize a moment of time:

> Allí estaba Simona, como insensata, cubierta con las añejas y pesadas joyas parafernales... que la abuela le había puesto poco antes de morir. Con el temblor de la niña, las joyas tintineaban... Allí estaba Conchona, la servidora fuerte y leal... Allí estaba Cerezo, el mastín corpulento... Allí estaban, sobre el ancho lecho de las nupcias de antaño, el traje de seda blanca brochada y el blanco velo (p. 61).

What movements there are terminate in fixed positions and the sobbing of Simona becomes, with its "modulaciones musicales" an operatic elegy. A tragic event is converted into its stylized depiction:

> Cerezo se tendió, al pie de su dueña, como en las piedras tumbales de las castellanas.
> Conchona se arrodilló a mascullar oraciones...
> Oíase el silencio estremecido de la noche.
> Llegaban a veces, ondulando como infernales banderas desgarradas, voces soeces de los criados cautivos...
> Cantó el ruiseñor.
> Simona se llevó las manos a la garganta y rompió en un sollozo, prolongado en modulaciones musicales (pp. 66-67).

The St. John's night episode in *El curandero de su honra* includes a section of stage dialogue that is doubly transposed: in his soliloquy, Tigre Juan repeats phrases and sentences from *Otbelo* and *El médico de su honra*; in a kind of play within a play, the hero delivers his own lines and those of others, amalgamating distinct roles. The passage brings to mind the Spanish *comedia*, not only in reference to the honor code but also in the subject of the monologues of Tigre Juan and Nachín de Nacha — the fugitive and illusory nature of life. By putting their thoughts into playformat, the author at once gives form to two traditional topics, "el gran teatro del mundo", and "la vida es sueño". The latter is then further elaborated in the novel's epilogue (*Coda*) where it appears as the dream of a hidden ever-silent creator: the poem with which the novel ends is a last variation on Calderón's famous verses. "Gozar... Penar... Vivir / Goces y penas huideros / Todo huye y se desvanece. / Vivir. Soñar. La vida es sueño. / No soñamos los hombres mortales. / Nosotros mismos somos un sueño. / El mundo es el sueño de Dios..." (p. 122). [6]

But there are other allusions to Golden Age motifs and the entire *Adagio* is rich in literary and theatrical reminiscences; the coordinating themes —honor, *libre albedrío*, the freedom and supremacy of love, the deceptions of reality— are not only inherited from the seventeenth century but are also developed with some of the devices of the period: the Cervantine comic anecdote (the peasant beating his wife whom Tigre Juan quixotically tries to save), and intercalated tale (Carmen and Lino), the echo of stichomythic verse in the parallel columns, the *conceptistic* word-plays, puns, paradoxes, and antitheses —indeed, the whole passage is like an extended artistic transposition. The literary tradition that provides the external theatrical frame —Don Juan, Calderón's *comedias*— is also the crystal through which the author refracts the climax and denouement.

---

[6] The topic is introduced early in the novel when Nachín de Nacha trying to induce Tigre Juan to join him in his spirit-haunted cabin, argues that the *duendes*, devils, and wandering souls with whom he communicates are more real than deceitful and insubstantial men; his rustically phrased *Beatus ille* declares man's fantasmagorical nature:

> Apartado vivo allí de bullas... No bien saco la pata de mi umbral, asiento la madreña en un país encantao, mano a mano con les animes y creatures del otro mundo, que es muy buena socieda... Tú no comprendes el canto del cuquiello, ni quieres creer en las xanas, y el trasgo, y el duende, y la huestia, y la santa compaña. Fías en cambio, y crees en los hombres. ¿No te desengañaste entoavía? Dícesme que todos aquellos espíritus que yo veo con mis güeyos y oigo con mis oreyes endentro de regatos y bosques, o bien se posan en el tejao de mi casa, o entran por el cañón, de la chimenea; dícesme que son na más que sombras de inorancia. Sombras, na más que sombras, son todos estos hombres y muyeres que nos arrodean. (*Tigre*, pp. 130-31.)

Conclusion: Theory and Practice

At the end of *La pata de la raposa*, the protagonist momentarily frees himself from emotional involvement in his own tragedy to view with detachment everything that happens — even what happens to him. He has achieved esthetic distance, and his feelings no longer interfere with an objective recording of events. In this new frame of mind, he is able to perceive the coherence and necessity of apparently chaotic happenings. Life, which in its immediacy is contingent and meaningless, is transformed into the orderly pattern of a work of art. Painful reality becomes sheer spectacle. Contemplation replaces desire and anguish (or, as Schopenhauer —the obvious source of these ideas— would have said, one is delivered from the Will by contemplating it as pure objectivity). To view the world esthetically is to protect oneself from suffering.

> Sus ideas y sentimientos adoptaban de nuevo la impasible serenidad estética. De actor de la tragedia, azotado por furias fatales, se había convertido en espectador que recibe deleite en seguir el encadenamiento de los hechos... Se había librado milagrosamente del desorden vertiginoso... estaba en la margen, tranquilo y sonriente, no contemplando en aquel raudo torbellino otra cosa que el juego de bellas fuerzas naturales... Alberto consideraba la vida como una obra de arte (p. 239).

Pérez de Ayala considers the novel and the drama as representations of universal harmony, condensed transcripts of the divine creation which embrace, at least by schematic or abbreviated reference, all antagonistic forces. The novelist reproduces the perfect equilibrium of reality by being strictly impartial and tolerant. He empathizes succesively with each character and then withdraws in order to observe their conflict — and ultimate reconciliation. We remember, however, that this ultimate reconciliation of opposites is evident not in direct experience but only *sub specie aeterni*, "más allá de la estrella Sirio". In some novels, the author tries to make that eternal order evident here and now, in the agitated existence of the characters. From outside the fiction, he decrees concord, and his creatures respond obediently, abruptly changing attitudes or reversing their direction. This is especially true in his last novels, *Luna de miel, luna de hiel, Los trabajos de Urbano y Simona, Tigre Juan,* and *El curandero de su honra*; in each, the conclusion is a happy uniting of lovers who, though separated for a time by unfortunate circumstances, were from the beginning fated to be joined. Opposites are reconciled not only in esthetic contemplation but also in the very action of the novel. In other words, the protagonist of *La pata de la raposa*, who is able to see his life as a "play of beautiful natural forces," is supplanted by the novelist who shows that balance of polarities within his own creation.

Artistic transpositions may serve, then, to convert lived reality into the stable substance of art. They are part of a general plan that organizes the welter of experience into a meaningful design. But they are also a way of pointing up the relativity of reality, its innumerable levels and refractions. The intrusions of the author, the abrupt shifts from life to art, sometimes freeze the action into the reproduction of a well-known work of art, but, in other cases, they contribute to a kind of joking dialogue with the reader in which both the real and the fictitious are combined, confused, and undermined. In all cases the author puts in the foreground of the work his own artistic activity. The perpetual vacillations between what things are and what we think they are is the coordinating theme of all the novels and stories. And the specific application of this theme is the novelist's own role, his free creativity. Instead of concealing his inventive function, he calls attention to it.

The interplay of objective and subjective is, of course, the basis of all fiction, but its precise demonstration becomes the aim of many novelists at the beginning of the twentieth century. European and American writers sought new modes of expressing and elaborating this elemental theme. In England, France, and America, the stream of consciousness writers developed techniques for an extremely subtle, illusionistic presentation of psychic processes, whereby the reader sees the world filtered through the perception of the character. In Spain, the novelists of the first third of the century (particularly Valle-Inclán, Unamuno, Pérez de Ayala, Gómez de la Serna, Benjamín Jarnés) chose the contrary approach — they externalized everything, willfully displaying the fictitiousness of their works and often depicting people as puppets in a comic charade. They broke the barriers between reality and literature by letting the character step out of the novel and confront his author or by using the art of the past as a mirror for their own creations (either an accurate mirror that embellishes or a concave one that grotesquely distorts). They delighted in the intentional display of fictionality, not so much in order to destroy the verisimilitude of the novel's action as to point out the ambiguous nature of the reader's own objective world. The confusion, duplication, and constant inversions of the two realms contaminate the external world and heighten the reader's awareness of the paradoxical, hybrid nature of his own manner of being. And in a world of infinite, unstable realities, the creative role of the artist becomes the one fixed point of reference.

Pérez de Ayala carried the narrative techniques of relativism to an extreme of conscious elaboration. His structural experiments are among the most ingenious and complex in the Spanish novel of his time. And his best novel, *Belarmino y Apolonio*, is a comic review and illustration of the novelist's problems and aspirations. How can we know reality and how can we represent it? The writer makes the technique of his craft the very subject of his work.

WORKS BY RAMÓN PÉREZ DE AYALA

La paz del sendero. Madrid, 1903. (poetry)
Tinieblas en las cumbres. Madrid, 1907. (novel)
A. M. D. G. Madrid, 1910. (novel).
La pata de la raposa. Madrid, 1912. (novel). Edition cited is in *Obras selectas.* Barcelona, 1957.
Troteras y danzaderas. Madrid, 1913. (novel)
El sendero innumerable. Madrid, 1916. (poetry)
Prometeo, Luz de domingo, La caída de los Limones. Madrid, 1916. (short novels)
Las máscaras, I. Madrid. (essays)
Hermann, encadenado. Madrid, 1917. (essays)
Las máscaras, II. Madrid, 1919. (essays)
El sendero andante. Madrid, 1921. (poetry)
Belarmino y Apolonio. Madrid, 1921. (novel). Edition cited: Buenos Aires, 1956.
Luna de miel, luna de hiel. Madrid, 1923. (novel)
Los trabajos de Urbano y Simona. Madrid, 1923. (novel, second part of *Luna de miel, luna de hiel*).
Bajo el signo de Artemisa. Madrid, 1924. (stories written between 1902 and 1912).
El ombligo del mundo. Madrid, 1924. (stories)
Tigre Juan. Madrid, 1926. (novel)
El curandero de su honra. Madrid, 1926. (novel, second part of *Tigre Juan*).
El libro de Ruth. Madrid, 1928. (essays taken from the novels).
Poesías completas. Buenos Aires, 1942.
Divagaciones literarias. Madrid, 1958. (essays)
Principios y finales de la novela. Madrid, 1958. (essays)

El país del futuro; *mis viajes a los Estados Unidos, 1913-1914, 1919-1920.* Selected and edited by José García Mercadal. Madrid, 1959.

La revolución sentimental. Buenos Aires, 1959. (stories written between 1909 and 1928?).

Nuevas divagaciones literarias. Selected and edited by José García Mercadal. Madrid, 1960. (essays)

Amistades y recuerdos. Selected and edited by José García Mercadal. Barcelona, 1961.

El Raposín. Madrid, 1962. (stories)

Tributo a Inglaterra. Prólogo de José García Mercadal. Madrid, 1962. (essays)

Pequeños ensayos. Selected and edited by José García Mercadal. Madrid, 1963.

Tabla rasa. Selected and edited by José García Mercadal. Madrid, 1963. (essays)

www.ingramcontent.com/pod-product-compliance
Lightning Source LLC
Chambersburg PA
CBHW021847220426
43663CB00005B/440